ANYTHING YOU ASK

Also by Colin Urquhart

From Mercy to Majesty
Listen and Live
My Dear Child
My Dear Son
Personal Victory
The Positive Kingdom
The Truth That Sets You Free
Your Personal Bible

Anything You Ask

Colin Urquhart

Hodder & Stoughton

LONDON SYDNEY AUCKLAND

British Library Cataloguing in Publication Data
A record for this book is available from the British Library

ISBN 0 340 74544 4

Printed and bound in Great Britain by
Clays Ltd, St Ives plc

Hodder and Stoughton Ltd
A Division of Hodder Headline PLC
338 Euston Road
London NW1 3BH

In thanksgiving for
the precious gift of
the Holy Spirit, who
inspires faith within
God's children.

Acknowledgments

My thanks are willingly expressed to all whom God has used to encourage faith in Him in my life. My prayer is that this book will be used by Him to build faith in others – and I know God will answer that prayer!

I praise the Lord for my wife, Caroline, and my children, Claire, Clive and Andrea. I am thankful for all their love and the encouragement they have given me in writing this book. My thanks also to Vivienne who has done all the typing, to Maureen for all her help, and to George whose helpful suggestions have been greatly appreciated.

The Biblical references in this book are taken from the Revised Standard Version, with the exception of the quotations from Nehemiah, chapter 9.

Contents

1

An Unbelievable Promise?

WE WERE SITTING having a leisurely cup of coffee when we heard screams. One of the boys came rushing into the kitchen: "Dad, there's been an accident." Charles didn't wait to hear any more. He ran out of the house and across the yard, closely followed by Joyce.

Caroline and I were staying with Charles and Joyce and their family, while I was ministering for a few days in Cornwall. On the previous evening I had been speaking about the prayer promises of Jesus and what it means to pray with faith, knowing that God is going to answer you.

We were already praying when Charles carried ten-year-old Joanna into the room. In the garage the children had been melting down lead to pour into moulds, to make gifts for Christmas. One of them dropped a cold piece of metal into the container causing some of the molten mixture to fly into Joanna's face.

Some of the liquid lead had gone into both eyes. Can you imagine the effect of molten lead on eyes?

It took her mother nearly forty minutes to remove all the pieces of metal. During that time we all prayed, silently and aloud, with Joanna and for her. But all the time we thanked the Lord that there would be no damage to the eyes, and praised Him for His healing.

Joanna was obviously in considerable distress, so once the metal had been removed from her eyes, we asked the Lord to give her a good sleep, so that she would not suffer from prolonged shock after such an experience.

She slept, and at 5 p.m. was downstairs having tea with us. Her eyes were not even blood-shot! And it was subsequently confirmed that she had suffered no damage to them at all.

That is our loving heavenly Father answering the prayers of His children.

Will He Answer Me?

Nearly everyone prays – at least occasionally. When they are feeling desperate enough. When things get so black, that God is the last resort.

For Christians, prayer is a way of life – or supposed to be. Yet for many it is a dull routine; for others an exercise that lacks power or reality.

"Does God really hear me?"

"Why doesn't He answer?"

Such questions are the symptom of a deeper unrest:

"Does God love me?"

"How can I be sure that He does?"

'Does He care about my problems?"

These and other uncertainties make it almost impossible to pray with faith, with the conviction and expectancy that God will answer. Many feel so desperate about their inadequacy in prayer that the cry of their hearts echos that of Jesus' disciples: "Lord, teach us to pray."

The Promise of Jesus

Jesus told His disciples: "If you ask anything in my name, I will do it" (John 14: 14). If you ask ANYTHING!

And the promise He gives: "I WILL do it." Not, "I may do it", or "I might", or "I can", or "I could". "I WILL DO IT."

At first sight those words seem so far from reality, as to be unbelievable. Yet Jesus said them and many like them, teaching that God wants to give you "ANYTHING YOU ASK".

When I ask church-going people if they pray, most say that they do. But if I go on to enquire if God does whatever they ask of Him, there is usually an embarrassed silence or even laughter at the very suggestion. People seem to be saying: "Oh we pray, but fancy expecting God to do everything we ask!"

And yet that is precisely what Jesus promises. Many of the things He says about prayer demonstrate that He knows His Father to be a generous Giver, One who loves His children so dearly that He *wants* to give to them.

This makes it even more remarkable that many Christians do not appear to believe that He is willing to give them whatever they ask. Some seem more concerned with discovering reasons why God should not give to them and meet their needs. Reasons, or excuses.

Jesus wants us to be an asking people. And when we pray He wants us to know that we can expect to receive *whatever* we ask.

He wants His Church to be a FAITH-FULL people! He is longing to see the faith that will release His giving into their lives. He does not want to speak words of promise that are disbelieved; for He is the faithful God, who keeps His Word. He always has, and He always will.

Here are three questions to ask yourself:

"How can I see the promise of Jesus fulfilled in my life?"

"How can I know that if I ask Jesus ANYTHING He WILL do it?"

"How can I pray and obtain positive results?"

The Roof on the Building

The answer to such questions is like the roof on a building. You have to construct the building before you can put the roof on. And before you construct the building, you need a firm foundation, the words of Jesus:

> Everyone who comes to me and hears my words and does them, I will show you what he is like: he is like a man building a house, who dug deep, and laid the foundation upon rock; and when a flood arose, the stream broke against that house and could not shake it, because it had been well built (Luke 6: 46–48).

When your life is built securely on faith in the words of Jesus, it does not matter what storm breaks, what difficulties you are confronted with or how desperate things become. For you will see Him bringing you through to peace, joy and victory over all such oppressive circumstances. You will know that the One to whom we pray is the God who is faithful. "I will not fail you or forsake you" (Josh. 1: 5).

However, Jesus warns:

> But he who hears and does not do them is like a man who built a house on the ground without a foundation; against which the storm broke, and immediately it fell, and the ruin of that house was great (Luke 6: 49).

People often believe they have faith, only to discover how fragile that faith is when put under pressure. They have never 'dug deep' and laid the foundation of their lives on rock. When the going grows tough they no longer know what to believe, or who to believe, let alone how to pray. The idea that they can ask Jesus for anything *and receive it* seems totally impossible.

Digging Deep

We are going to dig into the Bible to lay a firm foundation that will never move, no matter what pressures we come

under. We are going to 'dig deep' so that God can inspire
within us a faith that will not be shaken.

**Your words of faith: "IF YOU ASK ANYTHING IN MY
NAME, I WILL DO IT."**

At the end of every chapter, you will be given some words of
faith from the Bible. They are words God is speaking to
YOU. Say them to yourself over and over again until they
become part of you.

2

A Righteous Man

GOD WANTS A people for Himself. His own people. A people who belong to Him. Not because He is possessive, but because He wants to give to them. A people to love.

However, the rebellion, the sinfulness and disobedience of men had made it impossible for them to enjoy the relationship with God that He intended. Neither had they been able to receive all that He had wanted to give them. This grieved God.

> The Lord saw that the wickedness of man was great upon the earth, and that every imagination of the thoughts of his heart was only evil continually. And the Lord was sorry that he had made man on the earth, and it grieved him to his heart (Gen. 6: 5–6).

So God decided to "blot out man whom I have created". One man, Noah, "found favour in the eyes of the Lord". He is described as "a righteous man, blameless in his generation": the only man to be in right standing with God.

Although "the earth was corrupt in God's sight, and the earth was filled with violence", He would not condemn any righteous man to death. Noah alone was concerned to be a man of God, and his faithfulness was rewarded. God wanted to save His people; everybody else was too busy doing his own thing to worry about Him or His salvation.

Out of the relationship that he had with God, Noah heard his command to build an ark. God is going to "bring a flood of waters upon the earth, to destroy all flesh in which is the breath of life from under heaven; everything that is on the earth shall die" (Gen. 6: 17).

This does not sound like a God of love speaking; more like a God of destruction! And yet in the midst of this destruction God is to show His willingness to love and to save. His purpose is not to destroy but to give life. But, like you, God wants to see the end of all that is evil and unloving in His creation. He is the God of justice and as Paul was to write thousands of years after the story of Noah, "the wages of sin is death". God shows man the dreadful, awful consequences of rebellion, sin, disobedience and selfishness. They inevitably end in destruction, instead of the love, joy and peace that God wants to give to all His people.

A Binding Agreement

So to Noah, His faithful servant, God says:

> I will establish my covenant with you, and you shall come into the ark, you, your sons, your wife, and your sons' wives with you. And of every living thing of all flesh, you shall bring two of every sort into the ark, to keep them alive with you (Gen. 6: 18–19).

Here God introduces the idea of establishing a 'covenant' with Noah. A covenant is an agreement, a legal contract, a solemn pledge, a bargain, even. God does not *have* to make any such agreement; He chooses willingly to do so.

First, Noah must be obedient to what God tells him to do. "Noah did all that the Lord had commanded him" (Gen. 7: 5).

God, for His part, delivers Noah and his family from the flood and then establishes with His servant this covenant that He had promised.

> I establish my covenant with you, that never again shall all flesh be cut off by the waters of a flood, and never

again shall there be a flood to destroy the earth (Gen.
9: 11).

God gives Noah His word, which He will never break.
And the rainbow is taken as the sign, the continual re-
minder, of this covenant. From God's early dealings with
man we know He willingly commits Himself to a covenant,
to making and remembering the everlasting covenant,
"which I have established between me and all flesh that is
upon the earth" (Gen. 9: 17).

The terms of this early covenant are simple. God promises not to repeat the destruction of the flood. He has
demonstrated the awful consequences of rebellion, sin and
disobedience, and in the deliverance of Noah and his family,
He has shown His love and faithfulness to save those who
are righteous in His sight and obey Him.

Above all, God shows that He is not afraid to pledge
Himself to a binding covenant or agreement with man – a
word that cannot be broken!

Where You Stand

Today God still wants a people for Himself, His own
people. And He wants you to be one of those people, someone who knows that he or she belongs to Him. He wants you
to be His, so that out of His love for you He can give to you
to meet every need in your life.

Like Noah, you are surrounded by so much destruction
and violence, and it may be that you cannot understand how
God can love His creation, or why He doesn't do more to
end the world's problems.

You may be conscious of anger and rebellion in your
heart towards God, because you believe He has given you a
rough deal. You may feel so full of guilt that you cannot see
how you can ever get right with God, or why He should
want to give you anything.

You may have been a Christian for years, and yet you have never 'broken through' in your prayers; you have not come to that place of knowing that God is going to answer you.

God wants to show you that He does love you; He cares about you so much that He wants to meet you in every area of need in your life. He wants you to be free of anger, guilt and doubt. He wants you to be free to love Him, to pray with faith, knowing that your prayers will be answered.

In this book, He is going to teach you how to believe and trust Him, how to pray and receive the answers you need. He wants you to be one of His covenant people, enjoying His faithfulness and generosity, even when things seem at their most desperate.

Noah's Faith

Noah was a man of great faith. Out of personal relationship with God, he hears the Lord and believes the words that are spoken to him.

Believing God means acting upon His words. Not simply hearing them or agreeing with them. Doing them! Putting them to work in your life.

> By faith Noah, being warned by God concerning events as yet unseen, took heed and constructed an ark for the saving of his household (Heb. 11: 7).

That faith was amply vindicated, as the events that followed were to prove.

If we are to pray with faith, knowing that ANYTHING we ask will be done for us and given to us by God, we will need to believe what God says, and be prepared to act upon His words. That should be easier for us than for Noah. He had to hear God for himself and believe that what he heard was indeed the voice of God, before acting upon those words. We have the benefit of the Bible: God's Word spoken to His people over thousands of years; the revelation of who He is and what His purposes are.

Whenever we want to hear God speak, we only have to turn to the pages of scripture and there we discover words that are far more remarkable than those spoken to Noah. For God's promise to all His convenant people today is: "If you ask anything in my name, I will do it."

And that is only a small part of what He promises in His abounding, loving, generosity!

Your words of faith: "HE DID ALL THAT THE LORD COMMANDED HIM."

3

The Father of Faith

WE MODERN PEOPLE like to deal with facts. Presents us with a set of facts and we know where we stand. We have become very suspicious of promises. We are too familiar with politicians who make enticing statements, which are at best fond hopes; at worse, deliberate deception.

From early childhood, we learn to distrust promises. Human beings find they are easy to make; much more difficult to keep. As we enter adult life, we enter a world not of promises, but of legal contracts, binding agreements, often with penalty clauses if the requirements are not met. Everything must be 'cut and dried'.

God, however, has chosen to work in the lives of His people, by asking them to believe a series of promises that He gives them. But He is no human politician, or well-meaning, but unreliable, parent. By contrast, He is faithful to His Word – always.

So faithful that He does not mind incorporating these promises into a legal contract, a covenant.

Abram

> Now the Lord said to Abram, "Go from your country and your kindred and your father's house to the land that I will show you. And I will make of you a great nation, and I will bless you, and make your name great, so that you will be a blessing ... " So Abram went, as the Lord had told him (Gen. 12: 1–4).

Abram was a nomad, without a book of scriptures to teach him or a church to instruct him. Yet, like Noah, out of the simplicity of his personal relationship with God, he hears the Lord speak. And he knows enough about God not to argue with Him. If God says: "Get up and go!" you get up and go!

That is a good example of faith. Not only hearing and believing what God says, *but being prepared to act upon it.*

God promises to bless Abram. That means that God will care for him, will give to him and enrich him. He will make of Abram 'a great nation' and a blessing to others.

Abram, for his part, has to obey God and believe the promises that he is given.

> By faith Abraham obeyed when he was called to go out to a place which he was to receive as an inheritance; and he went out, not knowing where he was to go (Heb. 11: 8).

He would need to trust that God would lead him and guide him, and fulfil the words of promise that He had spoken.

The Covenant

The Lord kept His Word and gave Abram a land of promise. But how could He make of him a great nation, when he had no children by his wife, Sarah?

God's answer was to make a covenant with him.

> When Abram was ninety-nine years old the Lord appeared to Abram, and said to him, "I am God Almighty; walk before me, and be blameless. And I will make my covenant between me and you, and will multiply you exceedingly." Then Abram fell on his face; and God said to him, "Behold, my covenant is with you,

and you shall be the father of a multitude of nations. No longer shall your name be Abram, but your name shall be Abraham . . . I will make you exceedingly fruitful . . . And I will establish my covenant between me and you and your descendants after you throughout their generations for an everlasting covenant, to be God to you and to your descendants after you" (Gen. 17: 1–7).

Such promises must have seemed almost impossible for this old man to believe. And yet who can stop God doing what He says He is going to do? Especially when the promises given are part of a covenant, a binding agreement between God and His people.

Abram, for his side of the agreement must "walk before me, and be blameless". To mark the establishing of the covenant relationship, he is given a new name, Abraham, which means, "father of a multitude". And the sign of this covenant with Abraham and his descendants was circumcision. By this act, they are to pledge themselves to obedience to God, to be His people; and God will be faithful to them, fulfilling the promises that He gives.

No Laughing Matter

Not that God has come to the end of His promises to Abraham. He says that his wife Sarah, is to bear him a son. What a laughable suggestion!

Abraham fell on his face and laughed, and said to himself, "Shall a child be born to a man who is a hundred years old? Shall Sarah, who is ninety years old, bear a child?" (Gen. 17: 17).

When Sarah later overheard the news she too laughed.

The Lord said to Abraham, "Why did Sarah laugh, and

say, 'Shall I indeed bear a child, now that I am old?' Is anything too hard for the Lord?" (Gen. 18: 13–14).

At first, the things that God promises may seem incredible. You will be tempted to treat them like the statements of politicians. If only they were true! How different life would be! It is only when you begin to act upon God's promises that you discover that they are true and THEY ARE FOR YOU! Human beings are fallible; they fail constantly. God is Almighty and never fails. "Is anything too hard for the Lord?"

Abraham and Sarah both thought God's promise to be beyond belief – at first. Then they had time to consider who had made the promise, the One who always keeps His Word:

> By faith Sarah herself received power to conceive, even when she was past the age, since she considered him faithful who had promised (Heb. 11: 11).

> The Lord did to Sarah as He had promised (Gen. 21: 1).

That is the remarkable thing about Noah and Abraham and Sarah. In God's dealings with them, they discovered Him to be the God who was faithful to His promises. He kept His Word, even when it seemed impossible. If God said it, IT WOULD HAPPEN.

Giving What is Precious

Isaac was born to Abraham and Sarah, as God had promised. But the testing of Abraham's faith was by no means over. Isaac was the one through whom God's great promises to Abraham's descendants would be fulfilled. Without him there would be no descendants. And yet God says to Abraham:

"Take your son, your only son Isaac, whom you love,

and go to the land of Moriah, and offer him there as a
burnt offering upon one of the mountains of which I
shall tell you." So Abraham rose early in the morning,
saddled his ass, and took two of his young men with
him, and his son Isaac; and he cut the wood for the
burnt offering, and arose and went to the place of which
God had told him (Gen. 22: 2–3).

Oh the quiet submission! What is the use of arguing with
Almighty God? Was He now going back on His word? No.
Never. Abraham knew that God would still keep His prom-
ises concerning his son.

By faith Abraham, when he was tested, offered up
Isaac, and he who had received the promises was ready
to offer up his only son, of whom it was said, "Through
Isaac shall your descendants be named." He considered
that God was able to raise men even from the dead
(Heb. 11: 17–19).

God had given His word. God had entered into covenant
with Abraham, a binding agreement that He would never
break. If Isaac was to be offered in sacrifice then God would
somehow raise him to life again so that His promises would
be fulfilled.

Such was Abraham's faith. Because he knew the faithfulness of God.

At the last moment, the angel of the Lord tells Abraham
not to harm Isaac and delivers this message:

"By myself I have sworn, says the Lord, because you
have done this and have not withheld your son, your
only son, I will indeed bless you, and I will multiply
your descendants as the stars of heaven and as the sand
which is on the seashore ... because you have obeyed
my voice" (Gen. 22: 16–18).

God is the God of promise. The faithful God. He keeps

His word, even when that seems impossible; even when the circumstances seem to point to the opposite.

Abraham showed himself to be a man of faith, because he didn't believe the circumstances, he didn't believe the facts as they appeared to him. He believed the words of God and the promises he had been given.

Paul tells the Romans that the promise of God is "to those who share the faith of Abraham, for he is the father of us all" (Rom. 4: 16). The "father of faith".

You do not need to be overwhelmed by the faith that Abraham displayed. God wants to teach you to believe His words and His promises, to apply them to the situation that confronts you. Time and time again, you will feel more inclined to believe the situation, to accept that the problem is insurmountable, that God's promises could not be for you, that He will not change the circumstances. You will be tempted to believe that your faith is insufficient to see God answer your prayers.

"Is anything too hard for the Lord?" God asked Sarah. Apply those same words to all the problems in your life. You can struggle to solve them and fail miserably, over and over again. Then the problems seem like immovable mountains.

Remember that Jesus said:

> If you have faith as a grain of mustard seed, you will say to this mountain, "Move from here to there", and it will move; and nothing will be impossible for you (Matt. 17: 20).

Faith the size of a tiny seed. A very little faith. God asks: "Is anything too hard for the Lord?" His Son says: "Nothing will be impossible for you" when you have that tiny seed of faith.

Your words of faith: "IS ANYTHING TOO HARD FOR THE LORD?"

4

My Own People

GOD NEVER FORGETS the promises that He gives His people.
The descendants of Abraham left the land that God had
given them during a time of famine and went to Eygpt.
While there they became a nation of slaves.

> And God heard their groaning, and God remembered
> his covenant with Abraham, with Isaac, and with
> Jacob. And God saw the people of Israel, and God
> knew their condition (Exod. 2: 24–25).

In His love for His people, God wants to set them free
from their bondage. He calls Moses to return to Egypt,
where he had been brought up in the Pharaoh's court. He
had fled the country after killing an Egyptian who was beat-
ing a Hebrew, "one of his own people".

The Lord says to Moses: "I have seen the affliction of my
people who are in Egypt ..." (Exod. 3: 7). MY PEOPLE.
That phrase which is an indication of the special covenant
relationship that God had been prepared to enter into with
Abraham and his descendants. He would be *their* God; they
would be *His* people.

Moses, like countless others after him, thinks of all the
possible excuses for avoiding the responsible task that God
calls him to fulfil. The confrontations with Pharoah, the
plagues that were sent upon Egypt until its ruler agreed to
allow the Hebrews to leave the country, the Egyptians' pur-
suit and the miraculous crossing of the sea, these are all familiar enough. It is when Moses and the Hebrews had come
into the wilderness of Sinai, that God speaks to them again

of the covenant, of the binding agreement that is to exist between Him and His people.

> It is because the Lord loves you, and is keeping the oath which He swore to your fathers, that the Lord has brought you out with a mighty hand, and redeemed you from the house of bondage, from the hand of Pharaoh, king of Egypt (Deut. 7: 8).

The Covenant

Moses "went up to God" on Mt. Horeb, the holy mountain. Through him, the Lord says to His people:

> Now therefore, if you will obey my voice and keep my covenant, you shall be my own possession among all peoples; for all the earth is mine, and you shall be to me a kingdom of priests and a holy nation (Exod. 19: 5–6).

MY OWN PEOPLE. All the earth belongs to God and all the people in it: and yet He wants His OWN PEOPLE, who will be a holy nation, living for Him, obedient to Him. He wants them to receive all the blessing He desires to give in His generous love for them. "I will be your God, and you shall be my people."

What did God want of His people? What were they to do as their side of the covenant agreement?

God does not leave them in any doubt. He clearly and precisely gives to Moses the law, incorporating the Commandments by which they were to live. His people were to be obedient to the Law; then they would see fulfilled the rich promises that God had given them. He would be their God, to provide for them, to care for them, to heal them, to bless them. "MY OWN PEOPLE."

The immediate response of the Hebrews was: "All that

the Lord has spoken we will do, and we will be obedient"
(Exod. 24: 7). In this way they expressed their intention of
keeping their side of the covenant pact; they gave their
solemn promise to God.

The covenant was sealed with the blood of animals, which
was thrown on the altar and sprinkled over the people, with
the words: "Behold, the blood of the covenant which the
Lord has made with you in accordance with all these words"
(Exod. 24: 8).

Israel did not deserve to have the Lord as their personal
God, or to be His own people. The desire for the covenant
came from God, not from men.

> And he said, "Behold, I make a covenant. Before all
> your people I will do marvels, such as have not been
> wrought in all the earth or in any nation; and all the
> people among whom you are shall see the work of the
> Lord" (Exod. 34: 10).

God is not afraid to commit Himself to more and more
promises, for He has the power, the love and the faithfulness
to keep every one of them. They are set, however, firmly
within the context of the covenant. To see God's side of the
covenant fulfilled completely, they will need to be obedient
in fulfilling their side, of being a holy people who are living
to please God.

> You shall therefore keep all my statutes and all my
> ordinances, and do them (Lev. 20: 22).
> You shall be holy to me; for I the Lord am holy, and
> have separated you from the peoples, that you should
> be mine (Lev. 20: 26).

The Lord is saying: "You give your lives to Me, and I
promise that I will give Myself to you."

What an amazing offer! All that any man can offer to God
is a weak, sinful life. In exchange, God offers to him His life,

which is perfect love, joy, peace, healing, forgiveness and abundant provision.

> If you walk in my statutes and observe my commandments and do them, then I will give you your rains in their season, and the land shall yield its increase, and the trees of the field shall yield their fruit . . . (Lev. 26: 3–4).

God is concerned, not only with the spiritual lives of His people, but with their material needs and prosperity. He will fulfil His promises for these things, if they are obedient.

> I will give peace in the land, and you shall lie down, and none shall make you afraid (Lev. 26: 6).
> I will have regard for you and make you fruitful and multiply you, and will confirm my covenant with you . . . And I will make my abode among you, . . . And I will walk among you and will be your God, and you shall be my people (Lev. 26: 9, 11–12).

The wonder of it all! And yet God has something in store for all who believe in Jesus, that is far more wonderful.

God's Warning

But the Lord warns His people that if they fail to keep the covenant, if they are disobedient, the consequences will be dire. In love He wants to give to them and bless them; their disobedience stops the flow of that giving and blessing. So God will discipline His children for their own good, because of His love for them, so that once again they will be able to receive all that He has to give.

What if they do not submit to the Lord and return to obedience?

> And if by this discipline you are not turned to me, but

walk contrary to me, then I also will walk contrary to you, and I myself will smite you sevenfold for your sins. And I will bring a sword upon you, that shall execute vengeance for the covenant; and if you gather within your cities I will send pestilence among you, and you shall be delivered into the hand of the enemy (Lev. 26: 23-25).

That does not sound quite so good. God will warn His people before He allows these calamities to befall them; He will give them the time and opportunity to repent, to return to obedience to Him. For His purpose is not to afflict and destroy His people, but to be their God, who will live among them, providing and caring for them.

Yet for all that, when they are in the land of their enemies, I will not spurn them, neither will I abhor them so as to destroy them utterly and break my covenant with them; for I am the Lord their God; but I will for their sake remember the covenant with their forefathers (Lev. 26: 44-45).

God will never give up on His people! That is good news for all of us. He has not given up on you. You may feel that He is a million miles away, totally unconcerned about the details of your life and the problems that you face. It may appear to you that the only thing about God that you have experienced is His discipline.

But He has made a covenant that He will not forget. He warns Israel not to forget it either.

Take heed to yourselves, lest you forget the covenant of the Lord your God, which he has made with you (Deut. 4: 23).

These words are so applicable today. Many Christians suffer great difficulties because they forget the covenant that God has made with them – not the covenant made with Moses, but the new and better one given by Jesus. Some do not understand that they are in covenant relationship with God, and that he wants to honour every promise in their lives. Others long for such a relationship and for an assurance of God's love for them. He told Israel:

> You will seek the Lord your God, and you will find him, if you search after him with all your heart and with all your soul. When you are in tribulation, and all these things come upon you in the latter days, you will return to the Lord your God and obey his voice, for the Lord your God is a merciful God; he will not fail you or destroy you or forget the covenant with your fathers which he swore to them (Deut. 4: 29–31).

The Lord will have mercy upon *you*. He will not fail *you* or destroy *you*. His purpose is to give you life, His own life. He wants to meet *you* right in the middle of the tribulation you experience. He wants you to understand the covenant He establishes with all who believe in Jesus. He wants you to remember that covenant, to live by it and see His faithfulness in loving you and giving His blessings to you.

As you read this book, you can "search after him with all your heart and all your soul". And you will find Him. Because Jesus promises that: "He who seeks finds" (Matt. 7: 8).

Your words of faith: "I WILL BE YOUR GOD AND YOU SHALL BE MY PEOPLE."

5
Dismal Failure

WHICH IS THE better way? Obedience to God, or disobedience? That is the question that faced Israel throughout her history.

> And because you hearken to these ordinances, and keep and do them, the Lord your God will keep with you the covenant and the steadfast love which he swore to your fathers to keep; HE WILL LOVE YOU, BLESS YOU, AND MULTIPLY YOU (Deut. 7: 12–13).

But continually Israel failed to keep the covenant; although God remained utterly faithful to His side of the agreement. When the people were obedient, the nation prospered materially and spiritually; when they were disobedient, the Lord disciplined them. If they did not repent, He had to resort to stronger methods to bring them to obedience.

Repeated Disobedience

In Nehemiah, Chapter 9, Ezra summarises a whole period of history under the covenant:

> You are the Lord, the God who chose Abram ... You found his heart faithful before you, and made the covenant with him to give his descendants the land ... and YOU HAVE FULFILLED YOUR PROMISE, FOR YOU ARE RIGHTEOUS (Neh. 9: 7–8).

He then traces briefly the deliverance from Egypt, the crossing of the Red Sea, how God led His people through the wilderness and gave them "right ordinances and true laws, good statutes and commandments" (v. 14).

> You gave them bread from heaven for their hunger, and brought water for them from the rock for their thirst, and told them to go in and possess the land you had sworn to give them (v. 15).

Then Ezra begins to draw out Israel's great sins of presumption and disobedience.

> But they and our fathers acted presumptuously and stiffened their necks, and did not obey your commandments; THEY REFUSED TO OBEY, and were not mindful of the wonders which you did among them; but they stiffened their necks and appointed a leader that they might return to their bondage in Egypt (vv. 16–17).

Israel might be prepared already to forsake the covenant, but God had no intention of doing so!

> BUT YOU ARE A GOD READY TO FORGIVE, GRACIOUS AND MERCIFUL, SLOW TO ANGER AND ABOUNDING IN STEADFAST LOVE. YOU DID NOT FORSAKE THEM (v. 17).

God was utterly faithful even in the face of their disobedience. "You in your great mercies did not forsake them in the wilderness" (v. 19). "You gave your good Spirit to instruct them" (v. 20). "They lacked nothing" (v. 21). And God led them to the land He had promised them.

Did that lead to thankfulness on the part of the people, a thankfulness shown by a renewed obedience to God? Not at all!

Nevertheless they were disobedient and rebelled against you and cast your law behind their back and killed your prophets, who had warned them to turn back to you (v. 26).

Another time of discipline was necessary:

Therefore you gave them into the hand of their enemies, who made them suffer; and in the time of their suffering they cried to you and you heard them from heaven; and ACCORDING TO YOUR GREAT MERCIES you gave them deliverers who saved them from their enemies (v. 27).

God's Endless Mercy

The mercy of God is so immense; His patience infinite. If He dealt with us as we deserved, we would all be judged and condemned. He doesn't want that; He wants to forgive. He wants to heal and restore His people.

Sadly, many do not come to know His mercy until their lives are in such a mess that they cry out to Him in desperation. In His love, God hears them and answers them. He is listening for that cry that comes from the heart. He is looking and waiting for that turning to Him, even as a last resort.

WHEN THEY TURNED AND CRIED TO YOU, YOU HEARD FROM HEAVEN, AND MANY TIMES YOU DELIVERED THEM ACCORDING TO YOUR MERCIES (v. 28).

Many times they sinned, rebelled and disobeyed. Many times they cried out to God in desperation. Many times He had mercy on them, forgave and restored them.

And many times they sinned again!

So the same sorry process of Israel's failure to live by the

covenant is repeated over and over again. The only con-
solation in all this is to see the faithfulness of the Lord,
never rejecting the cries of His people but always honouring
His words of promise to them.

Knowing His faithfulness and mercy, Ezra prays to
Israel's covenant God, 'our God'.

> Now therefore, *our* God, the great and mighty and ter-
> rible God, WHO KEEPS COVENANT AND
> STEADFAST LOVE, let not all the trouble seem little
> to you that has come upon us . . . (v. 32).

At the same time, he acknowledges God's justice in the
way He has dealt with His people.

> You are just in all that has come upon us, for you have
> dealt faithfully and we have acted wickedly (v. 33).

That is the great difference between God and men. He is
always faithful. They are so often sinful, disobedient and
faithless.

Ezra prays in a time of crisis. The people are prepared to
return to the covenant that they had so often forsaken.

> Because of all this we make it a firm covenant and write
> it, and our princes, our Levites and our priests set their
> seal to it (v. 38).

But that was not to be the end of the nation's disobedience. Their covenant with God would be broken again,
and again, and again.

His Mercy Endures for Ever

As you look back over your life, it may appear to you like
the history of Israel, a story of repeated disobedience. He is

still the God of mercy. You may think that your disobedience means that you cannot expect to receive anything
from Him.

It is not His purpose to reject you, or condemn you. He
wants you to know His forgiveness for all your sins, your
failure and disobedience. It is that same gracious merciful
and faithful God, who sent His Son to establish an even
better covenant, with even better promises. He wants you to
be part of that covenant. It does not matter how disobedient
and sinful you have been, whether you feel a complete failure or whether your life is in a total mess. God will not reject
you when you turn to Him. He welcomes the repentant
sinner and orders heaven to rejoice over him.

**Your words of faith: "YOU ARE A GOD READY TO
FORGIVE, GRACIOUS AND MERCIFUL, SLOW TO
ANGER AND ABOUNDING IN STEADFAST LOVE."**

6

The Better Way

THERE HAD TO be a better way. But God did not abandon the idea of a covenant with His people. However, Israel's constant failure to keep the old covenant clearly indicated that an entirely new one was needed.

The New Covenant

In the prophecy of Jeremiah, God looks forward to the establishing of this new pact between God and man.

> Behold, the days are coming, says the Lord, when I will make a NEW COVENANT with the house of Israel and the house of Judah, NOT LIKE THE CO-VENANT WHICH I MADE WITH THEIR FATHERS when I took them by the hand to bring them out of the land of Egypt, MY COVENANT WHICH THEY BROKE, THOUGH I WAS THEIR HUSBAND, says the Lord (Jer. 31: 31–32).

God had been a faithful husband to Israel. He had entered into a covenant, a marriage contract with His people. But the nation had been like an adulterous wife, forever proving unfaithful, going in search of other gods, disobeying her husband, breaking His laws, deserting Him in favour of other pleasures. "Rejoice not, O Israel! Exult not like the peoples; for you have played the harlot, forsaking your God" (Hos. 9: 1). How will the new covenant be different?

But this is the covenant which I will make with the house of Israel after those days, says the Lord: I WILL PUT MY LAW WITHIN THEM AND I WILL WRITE IT UPON THEIR HEARTS; and I will be their God and they shall be my people. And no longer shall each man teach his neighbour and each his brother, saying, "Know the Lord", FOR THEY SHALL ALL KNOW ME, from the least of them to the greatest, says the Lord; for I will forgive their iniquity, and I will remember their sin no more (Jer. 31: 33–34).

"I WILL PUT MY LAW WITHIN THEM": Under the old covenant, the Law was written on tablets of stone given to Moses on the holy mountain. Under the terms of the new covenant, the law of God will be written on the hearts of His people. God would need to deal personally with each one of them to accomplish that.

"I WILL WRITE IT UPON THEIR HEARTS": The finger of God had written the Ten Commandments on stone. Only the hand of God could write His law on human hearts! "*I* will write it . . ." God says. Somehow God Himself would build His desires, His will and His purpose into those hearts.

"AND I WILL BE THEIR GOD, AND THEY SHALL BE MY PEOPLE": The old covenant promise is repeated. God still has the same intention. He wants a people for Himself; a faithful, loving people, who will live for Him and inherit all the promises that He has given. A people to whom He can give Himself. He will be their God, the faithful God who keeps His covenant and honours His words of promise.

"THEY SHALL ALL KNOW ME": Every one of the new covenant people will have a personal relationship with their God; they will "know the Lord". And that relationship will come about through the forgiveness of their sins: "I will remember their sins no more."

In the past, God spoke to the mass of His people through intermediaries like Abraham, Moses and the prophets. In the future, God will be able to speak directly to each one of His covenant people because "they shall all know me".

A Change of Heart

God would have to do something divine within His people, if they were to live in continual fellowship with Him. They would need 'new hearts', with the law of God written upon them. That calls for 'heart surgery' that only the heavenly hand can perform.

> A NEW HEART I WILL GIVE YOU, and a new spirit I will put within you; and I will take out of your flesh the heart of stone and give you a heart of flesh. And I WILL PUT MY SPIRIT WITHIN YOU, AND CAUSE YOU TO WALK in my statutes and be careful to observe my ordinances (Ezek. 36: 26–27).

"A NEW HEART I WILL GIVE YOU": God will take away the old heart, hardened against His purposes; the sinful, disobedient and selfish heart. Instead, He will give a brand new heart filled with His love, pulsating with His desires and turned towards His purposes.

A New Spirit

"A NEW SPIRIT I WILL PUT WITHIN YOU": Not only will God give a new heart that will desire obedience to Him; He will also make new the human spirit within His people. They will then have the inner resources to actually *be* obedient, to put into effect what the new heart desires.

"I WILL PUT MY SPIRIT WITHIN YOU": God will put His own Spirit, His own life, His own power, His own love, His own Being, HIMSELF, into His people. God will come and live in them, to *enable* them to be obedient.

When would God give His Spirit? With the establishment of the new covenant. In the time of Jeremiah and Ezekiel that is still a promise that awaits fulfilment. "I will put my Spirit within you, and you shall live and . . . you shall know that I, the Lord, have spoken, and I have done it." (Ezek. 37: 14).

This points, once again, to the fact that God will touch each life personally; He will live in every new covenant child of His. Each one will know that He has 'done it'.

"AND CAUSE YOU TO WALK in my statutes and be careful to observe my ordinances": Under the old covenant, God said: "You obey me and I will bless you. You do your part and I will do mine." That did not work because the people constantly failed to keep their side of the agreement.

Under the new covenant, God is saying. "I will live in you to enable you to do your part. I will do it in you. I will cause you to walk in my ways."

In other words, God is going to be the determining factor in BOTH sides of the agreement. When He left one side to men, there was continual failure. God knew there would be. He knew that the old covenant would not work and that one day He would need to send His own Son to establish the new one. But He had to prove to men that they were incapable of pleasing Him, of being obedient and faithful, if they depended only on their own human resources.

Under the new covenant there would not need to be continual failure, for God would be living within His people, enabling them to love, to obey and BELIEVE!

A New Marriage

A new kind of 'marriage' is envisaged. God will continue to be as He has always been, the righteous and just, loving, merciful and faithful Husband.

I will betroth you to me for ever; I will betroth you to

me in righteousness and injustice, in steadfast love, and in mercy. I will betroth you to me in faithfulness, and you shall know the Lord (Hos. 2: 19–20).

His 'wife' is to be like Him. A people who are righteous, in right standing and relationship with Him. A just people, who are loving, merciful and faithful to their God. How Hosea longs for the time when the people will 'know' their husband, will be bound in that new everlasting, marriage covenant with Him!

Let us know, let us press on to know the Lord; his going forth is as sure as the dawn; He will come to us as the showers, as the spring rains that water the earth (Hos. 6: 3).

"Know the Lord"

Those words are for you: "Let us press on to know the Lord." For the new covenant has already been established and God wants you to be one of His people.

He wants to give *you* a new heart.

He wants to give *you* His Spirit.

He wants to cause *you* to walk in His ways.

He wants *you* to 'know' Him.

And He has made all this possible through His Son Jesus Christ.

To try and please God in your own way will not make you one of His new covenant people. You will never be able to make yourself acceptable to Him, or work your ticket to heaven. He doesn't want you to think that being a Christian is living by a code of Biblical laws. A Christian is someone who has a new heart, a new spirit, with the Holy Spirit of God living within him or her. Someone who is 'betrothed' to the Lord. Someone who inherits all the rich promises that God has for His people.

As you seek Him, He will come to you "as the showers, as the spring rains that water the earth". He will bring an end to your harsh winter; He will water the parched earth of your life with "rivers of living water" – as you will see.

Your words of faith: "A NEW HEART I WILL GIVE YOU AND A NEW SPIRIT I WILL PUT WITHIN YOU."

7

The Separation Ended

THE PEOPLE OF Israel did not "know the Lord". Their sin, disobedience and rebellion separated them from God and from His purposes. That separation made it impossible for them to receive all the riches that He wanted to pour into their lives.

That separation had to be ended, at any cost. Even the death of the Son of God!

The Word Made Flesh

Jesus is the Word of God, the Word that existed before time began. God created through that Word. God spoke that Word from heaven to His people throughout the years of the old covenant. Some heard that Word for themselves; Noah, Abraham, Moses, Hosea, Jeremiah, Ezekiel, to name only a few. Others only heard that Word 'second-hand' through the revelation given to such men. And often that Word was deliberately ignored and disobeyed.

Under the new covenant, God wanted all His people to hear that Word for themselves, through His own Spirit living within them. Before the Spirit could come, the Word had to come in human flesh and then they could hear clearly what God was saying. They could hear directly, with no need for an intermediary. They could hear the promises that God wanted to fulfil in their lives.

The Word of God was coming to bring life to men, God's own life; to bring light into the darkness of the world, separated from fellowship with its Creator. God Himself was coming to live among His people!

Jesus described His own mission in these terms: "I came that they (men) may have life and have it abundantly" (John 10: 10). God's life, eternal life, "life in all its fullness". This is what God wants for His new covenant children: to know Him and to live His life.

To hear the words of Jesus was not enough to receive that life; these words had to be believed. To believe His words was to believe Jesus. To disbelieve His words was to disbelieve Jesus and the Father who sent Him.

> Truly, truly, I say to you, he who hears my word and believes him who has sent me, has eternal life; he does not come into judgment, but has passed from death to life (John 5: 24).

Would God's old covenant people accept Jesus? Would they believe His words and receive Him? Would they pass from the death of sin and disobedience into this new life?

> To *all* who received him, who believed in his name, he gave power to become children of God (John 1: 12).

To *all*, whether Jew or Gentile. All who received Jesus, who believed Him, were given power to become God's children. The old covenant relationship was between God and His people; the new covenant relationship is between a Father and His children, because those children 'know' Him.

Jesus came to reveal His Father by speaking His words and performing His works.

> The word which you hear is not mine but the Father's who sent me (John 14: 24).
> The Son can do nothing of his own accord, but only what he sees the Father doing; for whatever he does, that the Son does likewise. For the Father loves the Son, and shows him all that he himself is doing (John 5: 19–20).

The unity of relationship between the Father and the Son is obvious. Jesus is living in covenant with His Father, speaking His words and doing His works. This is what God envisages for all His covenant children; living in them by the power of His Holy Spirit; speaking through them His words of life; and doing in them His works of love.

So Jesus comes to lead men into the Kingdom of His Father. He teaches them to pray: "Thy kingdom come, thy will be done on earth, as it is in heaven." He demonstrates the life, the love and power of that kingdom, of God's reign in and among His people. He shows that God's will is all-important.

> I have come down from heaven, not to do my own will, but the will of him who sent me (John 6: 38).

That is the outworking of a 'new heart'; someone who does not want his own will, only that of his heavenly Father. That was to be finally tested in the Garden of Gethsemane, on the evening before the Crucifixion when Jesus prayed: "Father, if thou art willing, remove this cup from me; never-theless not my will, but thine, be done" (Luke 22: 42).

The Cross

Just as the old covenant was sealed with the blood of animals, so the new would be sealed with blood; that of God's own Son, Jesus. On the night of His arrest, Jesus had taken the cup while eating with His disciples, and said:

> THIS CUP WHICH IS POURED OUT FOR YOU IS THE NEW COVENANT IN MY BLOOD (Luke 22: 20).

To establish this new covenant relationship with His children, God was having to pay the highest possible price. Why was such a price necessary? Would it not have been enough for Jesus to come and speak the Father's words to demonstrate His works of love and power? No, because the separation between God and His people had to be ended, so that they could enjoy true union and fellowship with Him. So that they could 'know' him. So that they could receive the Spirit that God had promised and the new hearts that He wanted to give. So that they could become children of God and know Him as 'Father'.

Man's sin, rebellion and disobedience made him worthy only of death, of being separated from God. Jesus took that death-sentence upon Himself. The Sinless One dies for the sinners. The One who lives in union with the Father dies for those who are separated from Him, so that, through His death, they might be restored to that union and fellowship that God desires to have with all His people. The One who lives with his Father dies to establish the new covenant between the Father and His children; between God and those who believe and receive His Son.

Crucified with Christ

And yet Jesus did far more than die for men on the Cross. He took all sinful humanity to die with Him.

> For the love of Christ controls us, because we are convinced that one has died for all; therefore all have died. And he died for all, that those who live might live no longer for themselves but for him who for their sake died and was raised (2 Cor. 5: 14–15).

He took the sin, the failure, the fears, the doubts, the anxieties, the oppression, the grief, the sorrow, the pains, the diseases and sickness of men upon Himself and crucified them. He put them to death. And His resurrection proved conquered.

But not only the negative aspects of our lives were taken to the Cross. Jesus took us as whole people, body, soul and spirit, and put us to death with Him that we might become new creatures, raised to a new life in Him and restored to fellowship with His Father.

> Therefore, if anyone is in Christ, he is a new creation; the old has passed away, behold, the new has come (2 Cor. 5: 17).

The old way of approaching God and relating to Him has gone, has passed away. The old covenant is a thing of the past. Now, with the blood of Jesus, the new has come. And God Himself has done it!

> All this is from God, who through Christ reconciled us to himself and gave us the ministry of reconciliation; that is, in Christ God was reconciling the world to himself, not counting their trespasses against them, and entrusting to us the message of reconciliation (2 Cor. 5: 18–19).

It is this message that the world still needs to hear; that, through Jesus, a man can be restored to fellowship with God. He can know God and become His child and live in a new relationship with Him. He can be given a new heart, and God will put His own Spirit within Him, and cause Him to walk in obedience to His ways.

You Were on the Cross

Jesus took *you* to the Cross. "He died for all." And that includes *you*! He took you to the Cross because He does not want you to be separated from His Father. He wants you to know that His Father loves you, accepts you as the person you are, and forgives everything in your life that has been opposed to His will for you.

You are not accepted by God because you deserve to be, or because you have worked hard for Him, to make yourself acceptable to Him; but because Jesus died *for you.* He suffered your death-sentence for you. He experienced separation from His Father, so that your separation from Him can end. He took all your sin and failure and crucified it. He took YOU and offered YOU to the Father, so that your life can belong to Him and be filled with His love and power. You can share the personal testimony of St. Paul:

> I have been crucified with Christ; it is no longer I who live, but Christ who lives in me; and the life I now live in the flesh I live by faith in the Son of God, who loved me and gave Himself for me (Gal. 2: 20).

You will be unable to live the new covenant life until you have grasped this fundamental truth: GOD LOVES YOU AND HAS ACCEPTED YOU, because Jesus died for you.

It is a waste of time to try to make yourself acceptable to Him, because you will never succeed and because Jesus has already done it for you. It does not matter how sinful, disobedient or rebellious you consider your past life to have been; you are still made acceptable to God through the Cross of Jesus Christ. He died for *all* sinners. With *all* their failure, *all* their sins, *all* their disobedience and rebellion against God.

You cannot make yourself a child of God.

You cannot make yourself part of the new covenant.

Only God can do that. And He has made it possible for YOU, through the blood of Jesus. "This cup is the new covenant in my blood."

All?

Does that mean that all men are saved? That all are part of the new covenant? That all know God as their Father and are restored to fellowship with Him?

No, obviously not! You only have to look around you to encounter many people who appear to know nothing of the salvation of God, or the new covenant; who are unfamiliar with God and may even profess not to believe in His existence, let alone know Him as Father and live their lives in fellowship with Him!

These blessings await all who come personally to the Cross and appropriate what Jesus has already done for them. There is no other way to a new covenant life, but the way of the Cross. "No one comes to the Father, but by me," says Jesus.

But for every one who comes, there is a new life, a new heart, a new Spirit, a new relationship with God, a new covenant with new promises.

Your words of faith: "I HAVE BEEN CRUCIFIED WITH CHRIST."

8

'Lord, I come'

"How CAN I become a child of God? How can I enter the new covenant, with God as my Father?"

"By coming to the Cross!" is the short answer. By accepting for yourself what Jesus has done there for you. How?

Here is a simple method. It is not the only way, but it is thorough. It will clear the way not only to 'know' the Lord but also to receive the answers to your prayers. So even if you already know the Lord Jesus in a personal way, this chapter will be important for you. For it is crucial to understand how you can approach God, knowing that He will give to you and do for you, what you ask.

God has chosen to relate to His people through a covenant relationship, because He wants to give Himself to them. A covenant, however, needs two parties.

The Lord says: "You give yourselves to me and I will give Myself to you. You will be MY people and I will be YOUR God."

Entering the new covenant involves giving yourself to God; not only your sins to be forgiven; but *all of you*. Either you belong to Him, or you belong to yourself. Either you are His or you are not. Either you are His child or you are lost.

If you are His child, then you have come to that place of acknowledging to yourself, to God and to the world, that your life is not your own to do with as you like. You belong to God. You are His!

All of You

Jesus didn't die for part of you, but for YOU. He didn't take bits and pieces of your life to the Cross. He took YOU to the Cross.

Any housewife will know that one of the highlights of the week is the trip around the supermarket! Every time the same routine is repeated. You take a basket or trolley and begin to collect your groceries, item by item. Having selected what you want, you come to the check-out. You place every item from your basket or trolley on the counter and, as you do so, the assistant rings up the price of each on the cash register.

When every item has been accounted for, the assistant rings up the total and asks you for the money. Once you have recovered from the shock of how much you have spent, you hand over the required amount. You have paid the price for all those goods. They no longer belong to the supermarket; they are now yours, so you have the right to pack them in your shopping bags and take them home with you.

You don't select two or three items and leave the rest for general distribution! You have paid for the lot, so you take the lot.

God has paid the price for every part of YOU. Jesus died for YOU – not just the dirty, unclean, unsavoury, sinful, imperfect, failing parts of you. He paid the price for you as a complete person. And you were expensive!

Coming to the Cross is acknowledging, therefore, that every part of you belongs rightly to God. "You were bought with a price" (1 Cor. 7: 23).

You were already His, before you even thought of coming to the Cross. Jesus paid the price for you before you were born. It may be that in the past you have not realised or acknowledged that your life belongs to God, that He has the perfect right to do with you as He pleases. That is nothing to be afraid of because His purpose is to give to you, to be your

Father and to fulfil all His promises in the life of His new covenant child.

A token acknowledgment that Jesus is Lord and Saviour is not enough to bring about the real changes in your life that will enable you, not only to relate to God as your father, but to believe Him to meet you in every need, to answer every prayer.

Make a thorough commitment of your life to God. Here is how you can do it.

A Letter to Jesus

Make time to be quiet on your own. Have with you pen and paper. First, pray a simple prayer like this: "Please, Lord, show me myself as I really am and all that needs to be given to you." Then begin to write down everything that comes to you. Don't expect to hear audible voices from heaven; God will use your mind to show you what needs to be given to Him.

When I do this myself, I write it in the form of a letter to Jesus. That is more personal than a list of items. Such a letter may begin like this:

Dear Jesus,
I am offering you my life and this is what I am giving to you now.

You will need to write down both the negative and positive aspects of your life. I will list the kind of things that I mean, although when you write your letter, they will not necessarily come in the orderly way set out below. That does not matter. Nor do you need to write in beautiful English. God wants you to express what is in your heart.

A. THE NEGATIVE
My sins: Anything from the past that troubles you, even

things from childhood; your guilt and failure. Don't try to think of every sin you have committed; you would need a book for that, not a sheet of paper! The relevant things will come to mind.

My fears: Of people, of particular situations, of death, of the future, even your fear of giving your life to God. Don't try to psycho-analyse yourself, or impress the Lord with your knowledge of why you have such fears. Simply write them down to be given to Him.

My doubts: Doubt is spiritual disease, which you will never be able to resolve for yourself. Bring your doubts to Jesus that He might deal with them. Be honest with Him for only He can transform your doubting into believing.

B. THE POSITIVE

Many people bring the negative things to the Cross, when they first become Christians. However, many have never made a detailed offering of the positive side of their lives. Later we shall see how important this is.

My relationships: It is particularly important to give God any bitterness, resentment, or anger that you feel towards anyone, even if you have held on to these feelings for years because of hurt done to you by someone or several people. This is not always easy. In giving yourself to God, you are giving your feelings, the whole situation, with all the grief, sorrow, sadness and hurt that has resulted.

My marriage: Possessiveness can easily destroy relationships. Even your husband or wife belongs to God. Many marriages have been healed of deep tensions when the couple have acknowledged God's ownership of their lives and of each other.

My children: They are 'His' too. Often dangerously ill children have only begun to recover when their parents have 'given' them to the Lord, instead of holding on to them for themselves. God can take and fill, touch and heal, what is given into His hands.

My home and family life: God wants to fill your home with His love and praise. It will be a home where Jesus lives and wants to share His life.

My work: God is concerned about your working life. He wants you to prosper and know His enabling Presence wherever you are and in all that you have to do.

My time: Every day is a fresh gift from God, a day in which He can be honoured and praised in our lives; so the way in which we use the time God gives us is important.

My money and possessions: If Jesus has paid the price for you, then everything you are and everything that you have is rightly His – *even your money.* He is concerned, not only with how much you put in the offering on Sunday, but how you use all the finances and material resources that are His and that He makes available to you. Even under the old covenant, Israel only prospered when the nation was faithful to God in material giving to Him.

If you are already a Christian, it is important to give also:

My relationship with God: Your time for prayer, worship and studying His Word.

My life in the Body of Christ: If you belong to Jesus, you are part of His Body. He doesn't ask us to be 'independent' Christians, but "members one of another", sharing His life together. And remember, that church to which you belong is not yours to be run in your way. It is to become what God wants. So give it to Him. And give yourself to be used by Him to build up that Body in love and faith.

It will be obvious that the negative and positive sections are not exclusive. For example, in offering your time to God, you may become aware of ways in which you have been misusing it. That misuse will need God's forgiveness.

God is concerned that what you write comes from your heart; He is not interested in the neat way in which it is set out.

Why write these things down? For three reasons.

First: you will see clearly what you need to give to God, bad and good, in a way that is not possible by simply thinking about yourself.

Second: you will see yourself as you really are. That may not be very comfortable, for you may never before have been confronted with an overall picture of the awful truth about yourself.

Third: you will realise that the giving of yourself to God is not only something that you ought to do, or that He is wanting you to do. It is something you desperately need to do. Only He can accept you with all your mess (the sin, the failure, the doubts, and fears) and then transform you into someone filled with His love, His life and joy and peace; someone able to have his needs met, his body, soul and spirit healed, and his prayers answered.

"*Come to Me*"

What do you do with what you have written? One of two things.

Either: Get on your knees (if you are physically able to do that) and pour it all out to Jesus. Read it to Him. He is the One who said: "Come to me, all who labour and are heavy laden, and I will give you rest" (Matt. 11:28). That is a command: "Come to me". If you obey, His promise is that "you will find rest for your souls" (v. 29). You will find that He is gentle and loving and accepting.

Ask the Lord to forgive the sin, to set you free from the fears and resolve the doubts. Ask Him to heal you in any way that is necessary and to give you a completely new start to your life, with all the failure of the past forgiven, washed away by the cleansing blood of Jesus.

Ask Him for the precious gift of the Holy Spirit (see next Chapter).

And He will accept you, because the blood of Jesus has made you acceptable for fellowship with Him. He will forgive you. He will begin that work of salvation and healing in your life that is His plan for you. And He will give His own Spirit to live in you.

You will have a new heart and a new Spirit. You will be a child of the new covenant. And that means that all the promises of God are available to you.

Or: You may like to ask someone to pray through your letter with you. This should be someone whose confidence you can depend upon, and who exercises a ministry in the power of the Holy Spirit. It is not necessary to introduce this third person, but some people find it easier to receive assurance of God's forgiveness, or the healing power of Jesus, when there is someone to minister to them personally and to pray with them to be filled with the Holy Spirit.

God will answer your prayers and will give you the desire of your heart, whether you pray alone or with someone else.

God Wants to Give

Before you make this offering of yourself to God you may wish to read the next chapter about receiving the Holy Spirit. God wants you to give yourself to Him so that He can give Himself to you. He wants to fill you with His Spirit.

This is the way that He has chosen. We give to Him first, and then He gives to us. Later we shall see that this is a principle that runs through the teaching of Jesus: "The measure you give will be the measure you get, and still more will be given you" (Mark 4: 24).

God wants you to give Him your sins that He may give you His forgiveness.

God wants you to give Him your fears that He might set you free to trust and depend upon Him.

God wants you to give Him your doubts because He wants to give you a new believing heart and a new relationship with Him, knowing Him as your Father who loves you.

God wants you to give Him your relationships, that He may heal the wounds of past hurts and set you free to love and receive love from others.

God wants you to give Him your marriage, so that it can become a marriage filled with His love, where He is Lord, and a partner to you both.

God wants you to give Him your children, for He wants to be Lord of their lives and to give freely to them as He gives freely to you.

God wants you to give Him your home, so that He can fill it with His Presence and make it a place where people know the love of Jesus.

God wants you to give Him your work, so that He might cause it to prosper.

God wants you to give Him your time, because He wants to give to you as you learn to give to others.

God wants you to give Him your money and possessions, so that He can give back to you immeasurably more than you have given Him.

God wants you to give Him your relationship with Him, so that He can continue to give Himself, His riches, His blessings, His life and love and healing to you.

God wants you to give Him your life in the Body of Christ, in His Church, because through the love of His people He wants to give you joy in worship, fellowship and teaching.

YOU CAN NEVER OUTDO THE LORD IN GIVING!

We give of our poverty. He gives back to us out of His riches. We give to Him in our need. He gives Himself and His resources to meet those needs. We give, longing to be loved by God. He gives, longing to fill us to overflowing with His steadfast, perfect love.

We give ourselves. HE GIVES HIMSELF.

To me that is one of the greatest wonders of the Christian life. That God knows all about me, how weak and useless I am – and yet, He accepts me, He loves me and gives Himself to me.

What a God! What a Father to have!

Your words of faith: "IT IS NO LONGER I WHO LIVE, BUT CHRIST WHO LIVES IN ME."

9

The Holy Spirit

GOD WANTS TO give Himself to you. To live in you by putting His own Spirit within you. The Holy Spirit.

The promise God gives about the new covenant is:

> A new heart I will give you, and a new spirit I will put within you.
> I will put my Spirit within you.
> I will put my Spirit within you, and you shall live.

John the Baptist was "preaching a baptism of repentance for the forgiveness of sins" (Mark 1: 4). But He stated clearly that "after me comes he who is mightier than I" (Mark 1: 7). Of Him John promised:

> I have baptised you with water; but he will baptise you with the Holy Spirit (Mark 1: 8).

The word 'baptise' means to completely cover or 'submerge'. Those who came to John were submerged in water to show that God was washing away their sins.

Those who come to Jesus are not only to be submerged in water and cleansed of sin; they are also to be submerged in the Spirit of God and filled with His power and love. Jesus said:

> Truly, truly, I say to you, unless one is born of water and the Spirit he cannot enter the kingdom of God (John 3: 5).

Through the act of believing in Jesus, God gives us eternal

life, we are born of the Spirit and are given "power to become children of God" (John 1: 12).

> God so loved the world that He gave His only Son, that whoever believes in him should not perish but have eternal life (John 3: 16).

However, God's purpose is that we should not only be born of the Spirit, but that we should be submerged in the Spirit, enfolded completely by Him and filled to overflowing with His love, life and power.

The Counsellor

The disciples had become used to the physical presence of Jesus with them. The prospect of His imminent death caused them to be grief-stricken. Jesus assured them that they were not to be left to their own devices.

> I will pray the Father, and he will give you another Counsellor, to be with you for ever, even the Spirit of truth, whom the world cannot receive because it neither sees him nor knows him; you know him, for he dwells with you, and will be in you (John 14: 16–17).

They had known the work of the Spirit in Jesus's life and ministry and in the work that He had commissioned them to do in preaching the gospel of the kingdom of God and in healing the sick. The Spirit of Jesus, the Holy Spirit had been with them. Now the Lord gives the promise that the Spirit will be *in* them.

> But the Counsellor, the Holy Spirit, whom the Father will send in my name, he will teach you all things, and bring to your remembrance all that I have said to you (John 14: 26).

The Holy Spirit is the Counsellor, the Advocate, the One who will speak and act on our behalf. He is the Spirit of truth, who will teach us and declare the words of Jesus to us. That is of crucial importance.

If we are to believe His words and promises we will need the Holy Spirit to bring them to life for us. Only the Spirit can speak those words of Jesus to our hearts so that we believe them.

You can try hard to believe the words of Jesus and never make it. But when the Spirit declares them to you, He produces that inner 'knowing' that God means what He says and that He will do it. He will fulfil His promises.

> He will glorify me, for he will take what is mine and declare it to you (John 16: 14).

Rivers of Living Water

> Jesus stood up and proclaimed, "If any one thirst, let him come to me and drink. He who believes in me, as the scripture has said, 'Out of his heart shall flow rivers of living water'." Now this he said about the Spirit, which those who believed in him were to receive; for as yet the Spirit had not been given, because Jesus was not yet glorified (John 7: 37–39).

Out of these new hearts that God gives to His new covenant children, are to flow "rivers of living water". The Holy Spirit is not simply to fill our lives, but flow out from us. Not as a tiny trickling stream, nor even as a large river. As RIVERS. Rivers of love, life, joy, peace, power, forgiveness, healing and faith. Rivers of the life of Jesus.

But the Spirit of Jesus could not be given to live in God's people until Jesus had first given His life on the Cross, had been raised from the dead and had returned to be with His Father in heaven. He would receive glory, and those who believed in Him could then receive the Holy Spirit.

Jesus appeared to His disciples in His risen body.

And while staying with them he charged them not to depart from Jerusalem, but to wait for the promise of the Father, which he said, "you heard from me, for John baptised with water, but before many days you shall be baptised with the Holy Spirit" (Acts 1: 4–5).

And Jesus told them what this would mean for them:

You shall receive power when the Holy Spirit has come upon you; and you shall be my witnesses in Jerusalem and in all Judea and Samaria and to the end of the earth (Acts 1: 8).

"You shall receive *power* . . ." In Luke's account of the Gospel we read:

Behold, I send the promise of my Father upon you; but stay in the city until you are clothed with power from on high (Luke 24: 49).

To live as new covenant children is to live with God's power within us; it is to know Him as our Father, who loves us and cares for us. St. Paul says:

Because you are sons, God has sent the Spirit of his Son into our hearts, crying, "Abba! Father!" So through God you are no longer a slave, but a son, and if a son then an heir (Gal 4: 6–7).

An heir of all the covenant promises of God, both in the Old and New Testaments!

Receiving the Spirit

Jesus tells us to ask the Father and He will give the Holy Spirit.

Ask, and it will be given you; seek, and you will find; knock and it will be opened to you. For everyone who asks receives, and he who seeks finds, and to him who knocks it will be opened. What father among you, if his son asks for a fish, will instead of a fish give him a serpent; or if he asks for an egg, will give him a scorpion? If you then, who are evil, know how to give good gifts to your children, how much more will the heavenly Father give the Holy Spirit to those who ask him! (Luke 11: 9–13).

From these words of Jesus notice that:

1. We are told to ask and are given the promise that "everyone who asks receives".

2. God is not going to give anything harmful. He wants to bless and give life, not destroy us.

3. Even earthly fathers know how to treat their children properly and give them the good things they need and want. How much more will our perfect heavenly Father give us what is good? In fact He gives the best. Himself. His Spirit.

4. God *wants* to give the Holy Spirit "to those who ask him".

Paul asks the Galatians: "Did you receive the Spirit by works of the law, or by hearing with faith?" (Gal. 3: 2). Trying to obey the commandments of God will not result in being filled with His power. Trying to please God with our own efforts will not earn us the right to be filled with the Holy Spirit.

No, the Spirit is "the promise of my Father", according to Jesus. You receive the gift by hearing that promise for yourself, by coming to Jesus and asking Him to fill you with the Holy Spirit, to release the "rivers of living water" in your life.

And God will give you His Spirit because He has promised to do precisely that. And He is faithful!

Three Warnings

1. Try to avoid any preconceived ideas of what it will be like to be filled or baptised with the Holy Spirit. Don't look at other people or their experiences and try to be like them. God will do a unique, personal work in your life which will be just right for you.

2. Jesus does not say that you need any particular gift or manifestation of the Spirit to prove that you have received. He simply promises, "Ask and you will receive." And He adds, "Everyone who asks receives." He doesn't say: "Everyone, except you!" He says, "Everyone who asks!"

3. Don't look for particular feelings or experiences. Some people do have 'an experience', but many don't especially at the time of asking. Some people are tempted to doubt that God has honoured His promise and given the gift, if they do not have 'an experience'. Often they turn themselves inside out, looking for some hidden sin that could be the cause of God's displeasure and the reason for withholding the gift, when their real problem is that they do not believe God's faithfulness in honouring His Word. The 'experience' follows the believing; it does not precede it! When we seek the fulfilment of God's promises in our lives, it is not only a question of asking, but believing as we ask.

Prepare First

Do not ask to be filled with the Holy Spirit until you have done what is suggested in the previous chapter. You need to come to the Cross, before you experience a personal Pentecost in your life.

Or, if you are already a Christian, come back to the Cross and renew that offering of your life, and then ask to be filled with that "power from on high". God will answer you because He loves you and will give you what He has promised through His son Jesus.

God's Continual Giving

From time to time in your Christian life, you will find that God is calling you back to the Cross, calling you to a fresh repentance, to a new turning of your life over to Him. It is wise not to delay in responding to the Lord. He only calls us to a new repentance because He knows that it is necessary and will prepare the way for a fresh outpouring of His Holy Spirit upon our lives, a new release of the "rivers of living water" within us.

The disciples were first filled with the Holy Spirit on the Feast of Pentecost (see Acts 2). It was not long afterwards they were praying together and asking God,

> "Grant to thy servants to speak thy word with all boldness, while thou stretchest out thy hand to heal, and signs and wonders are performed through the name of thy holy servant Jesus." And when they had prayed, the place in which they were gathered together was shaken; and they were all filled with the Holy Spirit and spoke the word of God with boldness (Acts 4: 29–31).

They were filled again! As with those first disciples, those 'rivers' need to keep flowing in our lives. God wants those 'rivers' to be constantly released to enable us to love, to serve, to believe.

Your words of faith: "I WILL PUT MY SPIRIT WITHIN YOU, AND YOU SHALL LIVE."

10

The Word

DO YOU WANT to believe God, so that He answers *your* prayers?

Believing Him, His Word and His promises, can only come about through the work of the Holy Spirit within you. Because you are filled with the Holy Spirit does not mean that you will automatically believe and see the answers to your prayers. But the Spirit will "teach you all things, and bring to your remembrance all that I have said to you" (John 14: 26). It is the role of the Spirit to declare the words of Jesus to you.

Rock

So when the Holy Spirit begins to operate in you, the words of scripture take on a new meaning. It seems that they are addressed personally to you; they have relevance in your life. Jesus said: "The words that I have spoken to you are spirit and life" (John 6: 63).

The words of Jesus are not only for the times in which they were spoken or when the books of the Bible were written. They are words of eternal life, of eternal meaning and significance. "You have the words of eternal life" (John 6: 68), Simon Peter says to Jesus. Jesus Himself said: "Heaven and earth will pass away, BUT MY WORDS WILL NOT PASS AWAY" (Matt. 24: 35).

That verse is gold-dust! Do you realise that the words of Jesus are more reliable and dependable than the ground you walk on? You don't expect that to give way beneath your feet at any moment; and although there will come a time when the earth will 'pass away', the words of Jesus will never 'pass away'. They are for ever reliable and if we base our lives on them, we are on the firm rock that Jesus speaks of.

> Every one then who hears these words of mine and does them will be like a wise man who built his house upon the rock; and the rain fell, and the floods came, and the winds blew and beat upon that house, but it did not fall, because it had been founded on the rock (Matt. 7: 24–25).

Sand

If you are not on the rock, depending on the words of Jesus, you are on sand – and that is disastrous. The sand can consist of many different things:

The sand can be basing your life on the opinions of men, or your own opinions even.

The sand can be believing your own ideas of God, instead of what the Bible reveals about Him.

The sand can be depending upon having experiences of God. The experiences are fine. But if they are the basis of your faith, what happens when you have no experiences? God seems remote and distant and everything comes crashing down about your ears.

The sand can be living to please yourself instead of living for God and giving to others.

The sand can be always wanting to receive without giving first.

And what does Jesus say about building on sand? He says only a foolish man does that, and when the storm comes the house crashes to the ground, "and great was the fall of it".

During the early years of my Christian life I was taught that our reason was as important as the Bible. You came to the words of scripture and applied your powers of reasoning to it. As a result, you only believed what you could rationally accept as true and were free to discard the rest.

The outcome was a relatively powerless life and ministry.

Then I began to see the Word with the eyes of the Spirit. I began to believe it instead of criticise it! I began to accept it, instead of pull it apart so that I needn't believe it.

And the outcome was a new life and a new ministry in which I have seen the power of God at work in ways that I never thought possible, but in ways that GOD PROMISES IN HIS WORD.

Believing the Word

When you believe the Word of God, what He says can be translated into action, God's action in your life and in His world around you. The Bible stresses the importance of hearing the words of God and believing them. In the Old Testament we read:

> Hold fast to my words with all your heart, keep my commands and you will have life (Prov. 4: 4 NEB).
> Hear, my son, and accept my words (Prov. 4: 10).

It is for our own welfare that God is concerned that we heed His words:

> My son, be attentive to my words; incline your ear to my sayings. Let them not escape from your sight; keep them within your heart. For they are life to him who finds them, and healing to all his flesh (Prov. 4: 20–22).

It is through the words of God that we will be given understanding of His ways:

> The unfolding of thy words gives light; it imparts understanding to the simple (Ps. 119: 130).

Thy word is a lamp to my feet and a light to my path (Ps. 119: 105).

Being the Word of God in human flesh, the words of Jesus are words of life:

He who hears my word and believes him who sent me, has eternal life (John 5: 24).
The words that I have spoken to you are spirit and life (John 6: 63).

When He prays to His Father, He says:

Thy word is truth (John 17: 17).

Therefore: "Man shall not live by bread alone, but by EVERY WORD that proceeds from the mouth of God" (Matt. 4: 4). His words that God speaks to His children. And the Lord promises His disciples:

If you abide in me, AND MY WORDS ABIDE IN YOU, ask whatever you will and it shall be done for you (John 15: 7).

No wonder Paul says: "Let the word of Christ dwell in you richly" (Col. 3: 16).

New Minds

God does not want us to waste our intellectual powers of reasoning, so that we become 'mindless' Christians. God wants our minds and our intellects to be given to Him in order that they may become consecrated intellects; minds through which God can reveal His wisdom, understanding and truth. St. Paul tells us:

Be transformed by the renewal of your mind, that you
may prove what is the will of God, what is good and
acceptable and perfect (Rom. 12: 2).

Being a Christian involves a whole new way of thinking,
no longer seeing situations with a typically human attitude
but as God sees them. What for us seems an insurmountable
problem, is an opportunity for Him to manifest His love and
power.

There are so many situations that I encounter in which I
cannot understand the purpose of God, why he should be
allowing this particular set of circumstances to happen. I
have to remind myself of the scripture:

For my thoughts are not your thoughts, neither are
your ways my ways, says the Lord. For as the heavens
are higher than the earth, so are my ways higher than
your ways and my thoughts than your thoughts (Isa.
55: 8–9).

Our minds need a life-long retraining programme. But I
have learned to trust my Father in heaven and to know that
He never loses control of a situation.

Believing Jesus

We can be so thankful for the Bible, for the written Word
of God reveals His thoughts and ways to us. If we are to see
God answering our prayers then we will need to look closely
at what Jesus says about praying and asking. We will need to
pray in the way that He tells us, and see what He promises.
Those promises reveal what is in God's mind, what it is that
He desires to do in the lives of His children.

You cannot separate Jesus from His words. If you accept
the authority of Jesus in your life, then you accept the
authority of His words. If Jesus is your Lord, then His

words are precious to you. They are "words of eternal life". They are "words of spirit and life". And it is to the Word that you will turn for the guidance and the answers that you need.

This is not to say that the Bible is the sole means of God's revelation to us. We have already seen how the Bible can seem to be a dead letter without the work of the Spirit. And Jesus promised that his truth would be revealed by the Spirit. The Word and the Spirit belong together.

When the Spirit speaks the words of Jesus to your heart, anything becomes possible.

Your words of faith: "HEAVEN AND EARTH WILL PASS AWAY, BUT MY WORDS WILL NOT PASS AWAY."

11

The God of Promise

GOD WORKS BY promise in the lives of His children. Within the old convenant, He proved faithful to his words. Every time His people obeyed Him and fulfilled their side of the covenant agreement, they saw the blessings and prosperity that He had promised.

> Blessed be the Lord who has given rest to His people Israel, according to all that He promised; not one word has failed of all His good promise which He uttered by Moses His servant (1 Kings 8: 56).

Under the new covenant He is still the God of Promise. Those who live by putting their faith in His words shall see fulfilled in their lives all that God promises to do and to give.

Living by Promise

The great men of faith in the Bible are those who believed the promises that God made to them. St. Paul writes of Abraham:

> No distrust made him waver concerning the promise of God, but he grew strong in his faith as he gave glory to God, fully convinced that God was able to do what he had promised (Rom. 4: 20–21).

To live by faith is to live by the promises of God!

It is not enough to believe that God makes promises; we are only living by faith if we are trusting God to fulfil His words in our lives.

A Christian believes *in* Jesus. He believes Him to be the Son of God, our Saviour and Lord.

That same Christian may believe *that* Jesus can do today, by His Spirit, the same things that He did in His physical body nearly two thousand years ago. He may believe, therefore, *that* Jesus can heal the sick and perform miracles.

That still does not mean that he is believing Jesus to do those things in response to his prayers. He is only exercising faith, in the way that Jesus teaches, when he not only believes in Jesus, or believes *that* Jesus can; but *when he believes Jesus to do what he asks of Him!* When he acts upon the promises of God.

Faith

Faith is not only believing *in* Jesus.

Faith is not only believing that Jesus can work today.

Faith is believing Jesus to do it: to meet the need, to answer the prayer, to change the situation, even if a miracle is needed to do so!

How can we have such faith? And how can we exercise it when we have it?

> Faith comes from what is heard, and what is heard comes by the preaching of Christ (Rom. 10: 17).
> Does he who supplies the Spirit to you and works miracles among you do so by works of the law, or by hearing with faith? (Gal. 3: 5).

You are not necessarily living by faith, if you walk around with a Bible underneath your arm saying: "This is the Word of God, and I believe it!"

If you really believe the Word, you'll put it to work in

your life and then you will see God doing the things that He says He will do, the things that He promises.

Faith is:

Hearing what God says;
Accepting or believing it;
AND ACTING UPON IT.

All the Promises

St. Paul says of His brothers in Christ: "to them belong the sonship, the glory, the covenants, the giving of the law, the worship, and the promises" (Rom. 9: 4).

Christians are the sons of God. To them belong the *covenants* – in the plural. To them belong the promises. THE PROMISES OF BOTH THE OLD AND NEW TESTAMENTS.

Jesus does not annul the old promises that God had given to Israel; He came to confirm and fulfil them. But the new promises that Jesus gives are even better than the old ones! "The covenant he mediates is better, since it is enacted on better promises" (Heb. 8: 6).

St. Paul tells the Corinthians:

ALL THE PROMISES OF GOD FIND THEIR 'YES' IN HIM (2 Cor. 1: 20).

He came to confirm the old promises.

He came to give the new promises.

And His Father will honour all of them. That means that we will see them fulfilled in our lives WHEN WE BELIEVE THEM; when we have the FAITH to believe them!

Before we were Christians, we had no part in these promises.

Remember that you were at that time separated from Christ, alienated from the commonwealth of Israel, and

strangers to the COVENANTS of PROMISE, having
no hope and without God in the world (Eph. 2: 12).

Now that we are Christians, we are in fellowship with
Christ and "the covenants of promise" are our inheritance.
God desires to see His words fulfilled in our lives. He wants
us to receive His gifts and see Him meeting our needs. "Believe me," God says to us, "and I will do what you ask."

We are warned not to "be sluggish, but imitators of those
who through faith and patience inherit the promises" (Heb.
6: 12).

Note that both FAITH and PATIENCE will be needed.

Receiving the Promises

To read the promises does not mean that you will believe
them, or even 'hear' them in a personal way.

When you have a particular need, you may turn to the
Bible for help and discover many verses that are relevant to
your situation, including several promises. The problem is
how to believe them!

Sometimes the Holy Spirit does this for you immediately.
The words seem to jump out of the page and into your heart.
You may have read those same words countless times
before; now they are for YOU.

But it is not always so easy. And God does not want His
children to turn to His Word only when they have a particular need. He wants them to live by His promises continually, for only then will they be living by faith and trust in
Him. Somehow the promises need to be living words deep
within us. How can they be transferred from the head to the
heart?

A Simple Method

Here is a simple method of storing the promises of God within you. It is the way that I have found most effective and powerful not only for myself, but for many others.

First: take one of the promises from either the Old or New Testament. As a covenant child of God you inherit them all!

Second: sit down quietly in a reasonably comfortable chair and be as relaxed as possible. Spend a few moments letting the tensions of the day flow out of your body and mind. Deliberately allow your muscles to slacken.

Third: take a minute or two handing over to God the things that are of concern to you, so that these will not get in the way of hearing and receiving what God is saying in His Word. This is *not* a time to sit down and think about your problems. Just let go of them for a few minutes. You may need to ask God to forgive you and you may need to forgive someone who has wronged or hurt you.

Fourth: take the promise that you have decided to use and repeat it slowly to yourself a number of times. If you are on your own, you may like to speak it aloud, but quietly. This often helps concentration. Don't try to work out the meaning of the words in your mind. 'Hear' God speak them to you, to your spirit. Repeat the promise over and over again. 'Receive' it. At first, you will only be able to spend a couple of minutes with the one sentence. As you become used to this method of prayer, you will be able to concentrate on the same sentence for a much longer period of time. It is better to spend a few minutes, two or three times a day, than trying to 'receive' for too long at any one time.

Nothing dramatic is going to happen. Often you may feel that nothing at all has happened. But as you persist with the same word of promise for a week or more, it becomes part of you, and of your inheritance as a child of your heavenly Father.

Your words of faith, "MY WORDS . . . ARE LIFE TO HE WHO FINDS THEM AND HEALING TO ALL HIS FLESH."

Footnote As a companion to this book, the author is at present preparing a series of daily meditations, using this method of prayer, and describing how to use the Word of God as a powerful means of healing for oneself and intercession for others. These meditations will be published shortly under the title *Listen and Live*.

12

Old Promises

THE PROMISES OF God speak to your situation. He always has a word to meet your need.

As you read the Bible, you may like to mark or underline the promises God gives. They will be much easier to find again, if you do.

The prophetic books of the Old Testament are particularly rich in promises. God has often had to discipline His people; but He always gives words of encouragement and promises of abundant blessing, if they will turn back to Him and be obedient to His commands.

For many years I have been 'receiving' the promises of God. Here are some that have come to mean a great deal to me, many taken from Isaiah, (40–55), which are full of promises.

God's Calling

> You are ... my servant whom I have chosen, that you may know and believe me and understand that I am He (Isa. 43: 10).
> Fear not, for I have redeemed you; I have called you by name, you are mine (Isa. 43: 1).

His Love that is so personal for each of His children:

> You are precious in my eyes, and honoured, and I love you (Isa. 43: 4).
> With everlasting love I will have compassion on you (Isa. 54: 8).
> My steadfast love shall not depart from you, and my convent of peace shall not be removed (Isa. 54: 10).

Incline your ear, and come to me; hear, that your soul
may live; and I will make with you an everlasting covenant, my steadfast, sure love (Isa. 55: 3).

His Strength when I am confronted with my weakness,
which is often:

He gives power to the faint, and to him who has no
might he increases strength (Isa. 40: 29).
They who wait for the Lord shall renew their strength
(Isa. 40: 31).
I will strengthen you, I will help you, I will uphold you
with my victorious right hand (Isa. 41: 10).

His Forgiveness, which is constantly needed:

I, I am He who blots out your transgressions for my
own sake, and I will not remember your sins (Isa.
43: 25).
I have swept away your transgressions like a cloud, and
your sins like mist (Isa. 44: 22).
I have taken your iniquity away from you, and I will
clothe you with rich apparel (Zech. 3: 4).

His Presence, especially when confronted with a situation
that seems impossible:

Fear not, for I am with you, be not dismayed for I am
your God (Isa. 41: 10).
I, the Lord your God, hold your right hand, it is I
who say to you, Fear not, I will help you (Isa.
41: 13).
My presence will go with you, and I will give you rest
(Exod. 33: 14).
I will go before you and level the mountains (Isa.
45: 2).

His Faithfulness in bringing about the purpose that He has for my life and in honouring His Words:

> I will fulfil to you my promise ... I know the plans I have for you, says the Lord, plans for welfare and not for evil, to give you a future and a hope (Jer. 29: 10–11).
> My counsel shall stand, and I will accomplish all my purpose (Isa. 46: 10).
> I have spoken, and I will bring it to pass; I have purposed, and I will do it (Isa. 46: 11).

His Words of Encouragement when things are at their blackest:

> You will not be forgotten by me (Isa. 44: 21).
> I will be with you; I will not fail you or forsake you (Josh. 1: 5)
> Even to your old age I am He, and to grey hairs I will carry you. I have made, and I will bear; I will carry and will save (Isa. 46: 4).

That is a particular favourite when facing great difficulty. "I will carry you," says the Lord. Instead of battling through the situation in your own way, you can learn to let your loving Father 'carry you'.

His Guidance:

> I am the Lord your God, who teaches you to profit, who leads you in the way you should go (Isa. 48: 17).

His Promise for my children:

> I will pour my Spirit upon your descendants, and my blessing on your offspring (Isa. 44: 3).

His Promise for living in obedience to His Word:

> The word is very near you; it is in your mouth and in your heart, so that you can do it (Deut. 30: 14).

His Promise when I feel that I have failed the Lord completely:

> I have sworn that I will not be angry with you and will not rebuke you (Isa. 54: 9).

The Faith that His faithfulness inspires in my heart:

> The Lord is my shepherd, I shall not want (Ps. 23: 1).

And many, many, more. It builds my faith just to write them down again, even though they are so familiar.

The God who says all these things is my God, my FATHER. I am His child. And He loves me. So He will never deceive me. He will never speak false words or fail to honour them. He is faithful.

> I the Lord speak the truth, I declare what is right (Isa. 45: 19).

Whenever I put my trust in Him and believe the words He speaks, I see these promises being fulfilled in my life. That is what God wants; to see His promises being worked out in the lives of all His children, including YOU!

As you read the Old Testament you will find many, many more. They build your faith, because they enlarge your vision of how great your God is, and how wonderful His love for you, His beloved child.

Spend time 'receiving' them, as outlined in the previous chapter, so that they will become personal to *you*.

Your words of faith: Any of the verses listed above, particularly: "YOU ARE PRECIOUS IN MY EYES, AND HONOURED, AND I LOVE YOU."

13

A New Promise

YOU ARE A child of God, a citizen of His kingdom. He wants to see the words and works of His kingdom in your life. That will happen as you learn to pray with the faith that Jesus speaks of, believing the promises that He gives.

So it is with the prayer promises of Jesus that we will be principally concerned.

Asking Prayer

Asking is only a part of praying, but an important part because every day of our lives we have needs. Every day there are others for whom we want to pray, asking God to bless, guide or heal them.

Jesus died on the Cross to make it possible to know God as our Father. That privilege is not to be wasted. Because He loves His children, He wants to meet their needs; He longs for them to come to Him with faith, believing that He will give.

It is in asking that our faith is really tested, for Jesus tells us that His Father wants to give us *anything* we ask.

> If you abide in me, and my words abide in you, ask whatever you will, and it shall be done for you (John 15: 7).

The promise is clear; ask whatever (anything) you will (you want) and it shall be done for you. Not it may be, or could be, or might be, or can be. IT SHALL BE DONE FOR YOU.

It seems, however, that Jesus is making a condition: "If you abide in me, and my words abide in you."

In the Vine

It is the night of Jesus' arrest. Within twenty-four hours He will have been crucified and His body laid in the tomb. This is the last occasion before the Cross, when He can sit down with His disciples to teach them. He has already told them not to grieve over the events that are to take place, and has given the promise that the Holy Spirit will come to live in them.

He turns to the imagery of the vine and its branches to describe the relationship they are to continue to have with Him. "I am the true vine", He says, "my Father is the vinedresser", and you, He tells the disciples, "are the branches". They are parts of Him; they live in Him and cannot exist without Him. "Apart from me you can do nothing."

The purpose of every branch in a vine is to bear fruit. In the True Vine, it is only possible to be fruitful by 'abiding' in Jesus:

> As the branch cannot bear fruit by itself, unless it abides in the vine, neither can you, unless you abide in me (John 15: 4).

'Abide' meas 'rest', 'remain', 'stay', 'continually live'. When Jesus says: "Abide in me, and I in you", He means:

> Remain in me, and I in you.
> Continually live in me, and I in you.

If you do so, you will be fruitful. "He who abides in me, and I in him, he it is that bears much fruit" (John 15: 5).

You are in Jesus

You are already 'in Jesus'. You are already a branch of the True Vine – if you have acknowledged that your life belongs to God, if you have 'given' yourself to Him (see chapter 8). When you came to the Cross, you acknowledged that you were 'in Christ'. That is where God put you. You were 'in Jesus' when He was crucified, so that you might die with Him, and be raised with Him to a new and better life. You could not get into Jesus by your own efforts. You could not work your way there. You were put there by God Himself, so that you might live your whole life 'in Christ Jesus'.

So when Jesus says "if you abide in me", He doesn't mean "if you can manage to work your way to that very privileged position of living in the Son of God". Rather, He is saying, "If you go on living in the place where my Father *has already put you*, in Jesus, in the True Vine, in His Son."

His Words in You

Not only do you live 'in Jesus'; He lives *in you*. "Abide in me, AND I IN YOU." He lives in you by the power of His Holy Spirit. His Spirit will declare His words to your heart, so that you can believe them and live them out in your life.

Like a branch you are in Jesus all the time. You are part of Him, of His Body here on earth. You are 'in Him' like a page in a book. Without you the book is incomplete; yet a page without the rest of the book is virtually meaningless.

Stay in the book and believe the words that the Spirit prints upon your page, and the promise of Jesus is that you can "ask whatever you will, and it shall be done for you".

Don't look back on the failure of the past; look ahead with the eyes of faith and see what your life can become as you continue to live in Jesus and allow His words to live in you: a fruitful life, that will cause your Father to rejoice.

Hear His words:
Believe them;
Act upon them!

Much Fruit

Your heavenly Father wants to see 'much fruit' in your life. Jesus says that the Father 'prunes' disciples that they "may bear more fruit". He will cut out of your life the sin, disobedience and unbelief that hinder the fulfilment of His promises in you. And you will be happier without those negative, destructive things eating away at your faith.

Praying with faith, believing that God will do for you whatever you ask, is the kind of fruitfulness that God wants to produce in you. And remember, a branch cannot produce fruit by itself; it is the result of the flow of the life-giving sap within it. God has put His life-giving Spirit in you to make you fruitful.

Your words of faith: "IF YOU ABIDE IN ME, AND MY WORDS ABIDE IN YOU, ASK WHATEVER YOU WILL AND IT SHALL BE DONE FOR YOU."

14

Chosen and Appointed

HAVE YOU EVER wondered why God has chosen you out of the vast sea of humanity, to be His child; to love you and care for you in a personal way? It is a great mystery, isn't it? I never cease to wonder at it myself. What a mighty privilege to be chosen by God to belong to Him!

> You did not choose me, but I chose you and appointed you that you should go and bear fruit and that your fruit should abide; so that WHATEVER YOU ASK THE FATHER IN MY NAME, HE MAY GIVE IT TO YOU (John 15: 16).

There are four important points to notice from what Jesus says here:

First, a disciple does not choose to be part of the Vine; Jesus chooses those who will live in Him. He has chosen you.

Second, disciples are appointed to a task. They are not living in Jesus for a purposeless existence, nor to fulfil their own ends. God has not only chosen you; He 'appoints' you to fulfil a particular purpose.

Third, the task to which disciples are appointed is that of bearing fruit; God has chosen and appointed you to "go and bear fruit and that your fruit should abide".

Fourth, Jesus immediately links this fruitfulness with answered prayer: "so that whatever you ask the Father in my name, he may give it to you." This is the climax of the whole process. A disciple is chosen, appointed to a fruitful life in which God will give Him whatever He asks. This is the life for which God has chosen and appointed *you*.

A Fruitful Life

Imagine how fruitful your life would be if every time you asked God to do something He did it! And every time you asked Him to give you something He gave it!

Think how many people would be healed through YOUR prayers.

Think how many needs could be met through YOUR prayers.

Try to imagine the miracles that God would do in your life, and in others, through your prayers.

Consider how much you would be able to give to others if you received from God all that you asked for in *your* prayers. And that is precisely what Jesus has in mind! That you should have the fruitful kind of life in which your prayers are answered.

That when *you* ask, God does!

That when *you* ask, God gives!

Not so that you may be selfish and self-indulgent, but that your heavenly Father may be glorified.

> By this my Father is glorified, that you bear much fruit, and so prove to be my disciples (John 15: 8).

That is the ultimate aim of the Christian life: to glorify the Father. Jesus glorified Him by speaking His words and doing His works. All those who live in Jesus, will glorify Him by believing those words and seeing Him perform those same works in their lives.

Your Father doesn't want to answer only the occasional prayer, so that you are surprised when anything happens in response to your asking. He wants you to KNOW that when you ask, He WILL do, He WILL give.

The world around us will recognise us as disciples of Jesus when they see our prayers being answered. People don't want to hear our claims about a God of love; they want to see a demonstration of that love in the way He meets our needs. And God wants us to prove His faithfulness to the world, that He is the covenant God who keeps His promises because we, His children, believe them.

God Wants to Answer

God is love, He *wants* to give to His children. He *wants* to meet their needs, He *wants* to heal their bodies and minds. He *wants* to answer their prayers.

If you are a parent, and you love your children, you don't need any encouragement to help them when they are sick or have any need. Your desire is to give yourself in any way you can to help your child. Young children are sometimes easier to help than older ones, who want to assert their independence, to be self-sufficient and so may reject your desire to help. Sometimes you have to wait until they are prepared to come to you and ask.

When your child does come, are you going to reject him? Human parents may on occasions, but the Heavenly Father never will, because His love is perfect. He has given His Word that can never be broken; He will give to His new covenant children. He has sealed that promise with the blood of His Son, Jesus. And He will never deny that blood.

You are chosen and appointed to be fruitful. Your Father *wants* you to be, and He will give you every encouragement so that you can pray believing He will answer. He sent His Son to teach you how to pray with faith.

Your words of faith: "YOU DID NOT CHOOSE ME, BUT I CHOSE YOU AND APPOINTED YOU THAT YOU SHOULD GO AND BEAR FRUIT AND THAT YOUR FRUIT SHOULD ABIDE; SO THAT WHATEVER YOU ASK THE FATHER IN MY NAME, HE MAY GIVE IT TO YOU."

15

Have Faith

HAVE FAITH IN God. Truly, I say to you, whoever says to this mountain, "Be taken up and cast into the sea," and does not doubt in his heart, but believes that what he says will come to pass, it will be done for him (Mark 11: 22–23).

Have faith in God

You already have faith. The question is: in whom do you put your faith? A Christian does not necessarily put His faith in the Lord.

Your faith can be in yourself

There may be occasions when you do not consult the Lord about things you have to do, or problems you have to face. You may even feel good about battling through a situation on your own, without any help from anyone. A sad example of pride. You may not truly expect God to help, if you did ask Him.

Many ask God for help, particularly in difficult circumstances, when they realise that their own human resources are insufficient. But the substance of the prayer is often, "Help *me* do it."

Jesus emphasises the fact that God wants to work *for* His children; "it will be done *for him*." Jesus wants you to ask God to do things FOR you, to work *for you* in your needs. He wants you to know that He is so utterly faithful and trustworthy that He will not fail you if your confidence is in Him.

Your faith can be in other people

It is a temptation to trust people instead of the Lord Himself. You can look to some particular minister or servant of the Lord, believing that he will give you the answer to your needs. This is a particular temptation when healing is needed: "If I go to so-and-so, he will heal me." And if he doesn't work, then try someone else!

When a person has a desperate need, it is understandable that he will turn anywhere, to anyone for help. Understandable, but not necessarily the answer to the problem. Jesus says: "Have faith in *God*": know in your heart that He has not lost control of the situation, that He is more than equal to the need. That nothing is impossible for *Him*!

Your faith can be in God

The one person in whom you must have faith is your heavenly Father. He may use a human instrument to give you help, to meet a need, to be a vehicle of His healing power. But that human instrument is His answer to your faith in Him. He has chosen to answer your faith through that particular channel. "Have faith in God", Jesus says, not in the human instrument.

To have faith in God, is to have faith in His Son Jesus, who is God's Word. To believe Jesus, is to believe the Father who sent Him. Likewise, to believe His words is to believe the Father; they are His words that Jesus speaks.

In many situations, God is the only answer; a miracle is needed if the problem is to be met. You may think the word 'miracle' is beyond you; in which case you need "a mighty answer to prayer"! Your God is Almighty and promises that He will do anything you ask.

Faith and Experience

"But it doesn't work! There have been occasions when I have prayed and God hasn't done what I have asked. And I do have faith in God."

There is no point in having our heads in a cloud of spiritual unreality. If the words that Jesus speaks are true, then they can be tested by experience and found to be true! The difficulty is that often there seems to be a confrontation between the words of Jesus and our experience. When that happens, which is true?

The problem is not so clear-cut as that. The confrontation is not really between what Jesus says and our experience. It is between 'faith' and our experience. God's promises will *never* fail, when they are believed. Believing His words means expecting those promises to be fulfilled.

There are many occasions when we honestly think that we are believing and expecting God to do what Jesus means by this word 'faith'. There can be a great difference between our ideas of 'faith' and His teaching about it. It isn't that we need to have *more* faith, but the right kind.

The Disciples' Failure

When Jesus came down from the Mount of Transfiguration with Peter, James, and John, He was confronted with the failure of the other disciples to cure an epileptic boy. After Jesus had healed him, the disciples asked, "Why could we not cast it out?" He said to them,

> Because of your little faith. For truly, I say to you, if you have faith as a grain of mustard seed, you will say to this mountain, Move from here to there, and it will move; and nothing will be impossible for you (Matt. 17: 20–21).

Their failure was due to their little faith. And yet Jesus goes on to tell them that they only needed as much faith as a tiny seed and they would not only have been able to move this mountain, but that "nothing will be impossible" for them. Obviously the kind of faith Jesus was referring to, was different from the faith that the disciples were exercising when they were praying with the boy.

Mark records Jesus' answer to the disciples' question as being: "This kind cannot be driven out by anything but prayer" (Mark 9: 29).

Is Jesus saying something different here? No, in trying to heal the boy the disciples would have prayed, but their prayer had been ineffective because their faith was ineffective. It was not the 'mustard seed' type of faith that Jesus referred to. If it had been, the mountain would have moved when they prayed.

"Because of your little faith" and "this kind cannot be driven out by anything but prayer", amount to the same thing.

We may speak many prayers to God and ask Him to do many things. Do we pray with Jesus' kind of faith? That is the burning question. You can look at your experience for the answer. Where that kind of faith is being expressed in your praying, "nothing will be impossible for you." You may want to cry out with the father of that epileptic boy: "I believe; help my unbelief."

Jesus wants to answer that prayer, and teach you to pray with His kind of faith. "Have faith in God" can be literally translated: "Have the faith of God." The Lord not only wants our trust to be in Him; He wants His own faith to be in us.

Your words of faith: "HAVE FAITH IN GOD."

16

Moving Mountains

JESUS SAYS:

Whoever says to this mountain, "Be taken up and cast into the sea," and does not doubt in his heart, but believes that what he says will come to pass, it will be done for him (Mark 11: 23).

'Whoever' means 'anyone'. That includes YOU. Jesus wants that faith in YOUR life, so that you can look at the mountain before you and tell it to move – and it will! The mountain is that need, that problem that has to be met.

No doubt, we would all like to demonstrate such faith and exercise such authority. Are we wishing for the moon? Not according to Jesus.

Obviously it isn't a question of what words we use. There is no prayer formula to learn that will solve all our needs. Jesus warns about the meaningless repetition of words.

God is not impressed by the words that come from our lips. He is concerned about the faith with which we speak, with what is going on in our hearts. And so when Jesus tells us how the mountains in our lives are to be moved, He used the phrase "and does not doubt in His heart". It is not what you say to the mountain that matters, so much as what you believe in your heart when you say it.

Speak to the Problem

Many people pray about their problems; but not everyone talks to them! And yet that is what Jesus tells us to do. Speak to the mountain and tell it to move.

When I feel the early symptoms of an attack of 'flu or a cold, I talk to the problem: "Cold germs, I utterly reject you in the name of Jesus Christ. My body is a temple of the Holy Spirit and you don't belong here."

Then I speak to God in whom I put my faith, for He is the answer to the problem, and I praise Him for His victory over the infection. Sometimes the symptoms disappear very quickly. More often, there are a few hours of conflict but they do not develop as I keep trusting in the victory of the Lord.

Resisting cold and 'flu may seem only a small matter, but the principle is the same for bigger things in our lives. You will not have the confidence, the faith and authority to address mountains if you have not learned how to deal with foothills! As you see the victory in small matters, your faith is enlarged to trust God for bigger things. Why should our lives be disrupted even by colds and 'flu? We cannot prevent those infections being around us, but we can "fight the good fight of faith" against them.

Jesus tells us that, as we speak to the mountain, we must not doubt in our hearts that it will move. Once again, it is not a question of what you say, but of what you believe.

Dealing with Doubts

You cannot prevent yourself from being assailed by doubts. Sometimes they seem to come at you from all sides. In fact there are three main sources of doubt and you will need to know how to deal with each of them.

1. *Doubts come from others around us*: You live in a doubting, unbelieving world and many people around you will be full of negative talk and ideas, always grumbling and complaining. They do not have a positive faith that God will act in the circumstances of their lives; all they do is moan about them. Their ideas, attitudes and words can be contagious, and if you listen to those negative views instead of

the positive promises of God's Word, faith will very easily be eroded. You certainly don't want what faith you have to be disrupted by the negative attitudes of others.

2. *Doubts come from your own unbelief*: The more you look at the mountain, the higher it seems, and the more impossible to move. You can try to think of a way round it but you cannot move it. And you are not sure that God will either.

Many Christians are negatively-minded people. To 'think faith' requires a renewal of our minds and the whole of our attitude to life. That doesn't happen overnight. It takes time, and God allows problems in our lives to confront us with the doubting, negative attitudes and unbelief that we still have within us. It is important that as you become aware of them you bring your doubts to the Lord honestly and ask Him to forgive you and to inspire His kind of faith within you, by the power of His Holy Spirit.

3. *Doubts come from Satan*: He will try to sow seeds of doubt whenever possible, for he loves to destroy faith in God if he can. In scripture he is described as "the deceiver" and "the father of all lies".

The kind of thoughts that he directs at us are: "You don't really believe, do you?" "You don't have enough faith, do you?" "You aren't worthy enough for God to do such a great thing in your life, are you?" Satan is "the accuser of the brethren". No accusing thoughts come from the Holy Spirit, but from the one who wants to destroy faith.

Paul says that we are to take "the shield of faith, with which you can quench all the flaming darts of the evil one" (Eph. 6: 16), all those lying, deceiving, accusations. James says: "Resist the devil and he will flee from you" (James 4.7).

Hold on to the promises that your Father gives to you as His new covenant child and refuse to accept any of the enemy's lies.

So the attacks on our faith are threefold:
From the negative attitudes around us.

From our own doubting.

From the one who loves to destroy faith.

In other words, the world, the flesh and the devil.

Instead of this doubt, Jesus says that the man who speaks to the mountain with faith "believes that what he says will come to pass". He is not speaking and *hoping* that the problem will go away. He *knows* that it will! He appreciates that God does not want that mountain there, any more than he does.

God Wants the Mountains Moved

Now this is where we come up against a major problem. Many Christians are brought up to believe that God wants them to have mountains, insurmountable problems and difficulties. Jesus would hardly teach us to exercise faith to remove them if all the time God wanted us to be stuck with them!

It is easy to give in to a situation, if you know in your heart that you do not have the faith to see the mountain moved. You are tempted to look for an excuse for it to stay. You may start using such phrases as:

"God is teaching me something through it."

"It is the cross I have to carry!"

"There are others worse off than me."

It is true that God teaches us through all the circumstances of our lives, and that the mountains would not be there unless He allowed them. But His purpose is to give life, not destroy it or make it almost unbearable for His people. He wants to see the faith in His children that will believe the mountains to move, not be left there.

If you think that your problems are your cross, then you are carrying the wrong one. Jesus died on His Cross to save you from all that is negative – sin, disease, fear and death. The cross that Jesus tells us to carry is the one that we willingly take up for ourselves – not problems that we don't want. It is the cross of self-denial in order that we might live for the glory of the Father and the good of His kingdom. "If any man would come after me, let him deny himself and take up his cross and follow me" (Matt. 16: 24).

There may be many others who are worse off than yourself. That does not alter the fact that God wants to meet every need in your life. St. Paul was not afraid to say to the Philippians:

> My God will supply every need of yours according to his riches in glory in Christ Jesus (Phil. 4: 19).

He is your God too and these words are addressed to you. The fact that God meets every need in your life will not take away from His giving to others. God is prepared to meet every need, not out of limited human resources, but "according to his riches in glory in Christ Jesus". And those riches are inexhaustible! You will never come to the end of what God is prepared to give you through His Son.

No Excuses

Perhaps the most common excuses are: "I am not worthy", and "Your will, not mine be done, O Lord".

Of ourselves, none of us is worthy to receive anything from God. But through the Cross of Jesus we are made worthy. So you can say: "Of myself I am unworthy, but God has made me worthy to receive His riches through the blood of His Son, Jesus. God loves me; He has accepted me; and He wants to give to me. He wants to meet '*every need*' of mine 'according to his riches in glory in Christ Jesus'. I am one of His new covenant children."

Jesus' prayer: "nevertheless not my will, but thine, be done," is so often misused by Christians when they pray. It is the prayer of submission that Jesus prayed in the Garden of Gethsemane immediately before His arrest, prior to the crucifixion.

Jesus already knew the will of His Father when He prayed it. He knew that He had come to Jerusalem and there would "suffer many things from the elders and chief priests and scribes, and be killed and on the third day be raised" (Matt. 16: 21). He had repeatedly warned the disciples of these things. He wanted His father's purpose to be worked out in some other way, if at all possible. But He was not prepared to allow His will to come into conflict with His Father's plan. So He submitted to what He knew His Father was asking of Him. He was denying Himself for the sake of God's kingdom.

His prayer is only appropriate for you when you need to submit to something that God is asking of you that you do not want for yourself. They are not appropriate words to tack on to the end of every prayer in which you ask God to do something. When used in such a way they often indicate that you don't really believe that God will do what you ask. If the prayer is not answered in the way you want, then you can say: "It obviously wasn't the Lord's will." Then you won't have to face uncomfortable questions, such as:

"Did I really believe when I prayed?"

"Did I expect God to do it?"

"Did I persist in my prayer?"

There are many situations when we pray, but don't see the desired result, not because God did not want to answer, but because we did not pray with faith and persistence – as Jesus tells us to!

There is so much in scripture that shows us that God does want to heal us and meet our needs, He wants the mountains moved. We don't need to pray "if it be thy will" in such situations. Instead we need the faith to make God's will effective.

God loves you as one of His new covenant children and He wants that mountain moved. In fact, He will be blessed when it is moved and so will you. So Jesus wants you to speak to your mountains and believe that what you say will come to pass. And what is His promise if you do? "It will be done *for you.*"

He does not say that you have to move the mountain. You have to speak to it, believe that it will move, and it will be done for you. God is the One who will move it – not you.

You speak,
You believe,
God moves the mountain for you.

Your words of faith: "NOTHING WILL BE IMPOSSIBLE FOR YOU."

17

The Prayer of Faith

HOW ARE WE to ask? Jesus says:

> Therefore I tell you, whatever you ask in prayer, believe that you have received it, and it will be yours (Mark 11: 24).

You not only speak to the mountain, believing it will move. You also speak to God, believing that you have received what you ask. And Jesus says: "it will be yours." You speak to the God of promise, who always keeps His word.

'Whatever' here, literally means, 'all things'. All the things that you ask God in prayer to give you 'will be yours'. When you ask, you are to believe that you have already received the answer to your prayer. You can only believe like that, if you know that God wants to give you that particular thing for which you ask, if the spirit witnesses that truth to your heart.

That is why it has been so important to dig a 'firm foundation', before looking at these prayer promises. You will not find it easy to believe that you have already received it unless you know the utter faithfulness of God in keeping all the words of the covenant that He has established with His children.

Of His own choice, God has put Himself in the position of binding Himself by His Word. He has sealed the covenant with the blood of His Son, Jesus. He *must* do what He has promised. That is no problem for Him, because He wants to keep His promises. He would not have made them otherwise.

They are applicable to all the new covenant children of God. He has made you His child because He loves you; He wants to bless you and pour His riches into your life. He has accepted you through the blood of His Son, Jesus. The Cross removes any hindrance there may be to receiving what God has to give you and also provides the victory over every manifestation of evil. He wants to answer your prayers.

God has given you the power of the Holy Spirit to inspire faith in you, the faith that Jesus talks about, and to reveal His Word to you so that you can act upon it.

God will Answer

We have already discovered twenty good reasons why God wants to answer your prayers.

1. God is faithful.
2. He makes an everlasting covenant with His children.
3. He keeps all the promises of that covenant.
4. He seals the covenant with the blood of Jesus; His words cannot be broken.
5. He loves you.
6. He has accepted *you* as His child of the new covenant.
7. He is your Father. *You* belong to Him.
8. He gives *you* promises as your inheritance as His child.
9. He wants to bless *you.*
10. He wants to give to *you.*
11. He wants to meet *every need* in your life.
12. He wants to move the mountains.
13. He wants to heal *you* in body, soul and spirit.
14. He has given *you* His Holy Spirit to live in you.
15. He wants to inspire faith in *you* by His Spirit.
16. He wants *you* to ask and pray.
17. He wants to answer your prayers.
18. He wants to be glorified in giving to *you.*

19. He wants your joy to be full as you receive.
20. He wants others to see that you are His disciples, because much fruit is produced from your prayers.

These are twenty good reasons for praying. Twenty good reasons for asking. Twenty good reasons for believing that when you ask, God will answer: "If you ask anything in my name, I will do it."

When these truths begin to take hold of your heart, you will realise that you can dare to EXPECT answers to your prayer. Not to some of them; to *all* of them.

We often say God is 'almighty' and so He is! That means that He is all-powerful. Nothing is too great or too hard for Him. Jesus teaches us that anything is possible for someone who has faith; that 'mountain-moving' faith of which He speaks.

St. Paul talks of "the immeasurable greatness of his power in us who believe, according to the working of his great might" (Eph. 1: 19): a power so great that it cannot be measured. In us who *believe*.

He is ALMIGHTY. That is reason No. 21 for asking! Nothing is beyond Him. And yet so often we come to Him full of fears and doubts.

"Will He do it?"

"Does He really want to?"

"Does He love me enough?"

Ask With Confidence

Jesus wants you to approach your Father with confidence; not expecting *any* answer, but believing that He will do what you ask.

Where in His teaching does Jesus tell us to expect the answer: 'No'?

Nowhere!

As we approach the Lord in prayer, it is natural that we

should want to stand before Him with heads bowed, because we have sinned and we need to be forgiven. When we have confessed and received His forgiveness, He doesn't want us to continue to stand 'afar off' looking crestfallen.

We are forgiven!

So we can look up, as Jesus did when He prayed expectantly to His Father. He knew that He would always honour His prayer, because He is faithful. "And Jesus lifted up his eyes and said, 'Father, I thank thee that thou hast heard me. I know that thou hearest me always' " (John 11: 41–42). He said those words before He commanded Lazarus to come out of the tomb, where he had been buried for four days. Jesus obviously believed that He had received the answer to His prayer, even before He asked.

When He ministered to those who came with their needs, we see Him talking to the mountains, knowing that His Father's works would be accomplished.

That is how God wants us to approach life, full of expectancy that God is going to be at work in every situation as we release our faith in Him. With a God like ours, with a Father like our heavenly Father, we can dare to believe that we have already received it when we ask, because He will be faithful in giving to us. "It will be yours", says Jesus.

When 'Faith' is Not Faith

"Father, we bring before you our dear sister, Agatha, who has been given only a few weeks to live by her doctor. We praise you that you love her and that you are the Lord our Healer. We ask you now, in the name of Jesus, to lay your hand upon her and heal her. We thank you for your promise; and we claim that promise now. We thank you that it is done for your glory. Thank you, Father."

And everybody says: "Amen".

It sounds impressive! It seems that the person praying really believes that the Lord's healing gift for Agatha has already been received. However, after the meeting the same voice which uttered this 'prayer of faith' is overheard saying to a friend: "Poor old Agatha. Her husband, Bert, will be very lonely without her!"

What does that person really believe: the impressive words of that prayer or the remarks made afterwards? The two are inconsistent. The people saying 'Amen' may have 'believed' many different things.

"I was hoping the Lord would take the pain away."

"I was praying that she would have a quick and peaceful death."

"I was thinking of poor Bert. He won't know how to cope on his own!"

"I was thinking of dear Amy who died of the same disease only last month."

"I was trying to believe."

"I was imagining her getting out of bed, healed by God."

"I could see Jesus standing by her and comforting her."

A variety of attitudes, some displaying a measure of faith; yet many negative and certainly not the prayer of faith.

Your faith, what you really believe, is seen as much in your conversation with other people, as in your conversation with God. You believe what you say to others, no matter what words you speak during your time of prayer.

How Would God Answer?

Put yourself in God's position, wanting to heal Agatha and waiting to see the faith that will release your healing into her life. How would you answer this situation? Remember that under the terms of the covenant you will keep your promises but your children are expected to believe them, to believe that they have already received what they ask.

Would you not want to show your children that they are not truly believing you? They are saying the right words, but by no means all of them have faith-full, expectant attitudes. Most would be more than a little surprised if Agatha were healed.

> Let him ask in faith, with no doubting, for he who doubts is like a wave of the sea that is driven and tossed by the wind. For that person must not suppose that a double-minded man, unstable in all his ways, will receive anything from the Lord (James 1: 6–8).

Know What You Believe

Before I ask God to do or give something, I ask myself a question: "Colin, what are you expecting the Lord to do as a result of this prayer?" I have be be honest with myself. It is not a question of how I would like Him to answer, or what I hope He will do; but what I *believe* that He will certainly do. What I KNOW IN MY HEART HE WILL DO.

Sometimes I am well aware that I do not really believe God for the answer that will meet the need. I want to, but I don't. I have to confess my doubt and ask the Lord to inspire, by His Spirit, the faith that is lacking.

God has promised to do what we believe. In His generosity, He is likely to do much more, but He has pledged Himself, as our covenant God, to do whatever we believe He will do.

Be Specific

If you are praying with faith, expecting God to answer you, then you will be specific in what you ask. Vague prayers are the expression of vague faith. Those who pray vague prayers are not sure what they believe.

How can you "believe that you have received it", if you are not sure what you are asking God to do? Before you can be specific with God, you need to be clear in your own mind as to what you are believing.

Those who pray vaguely are pleased with any answer they receive. "That must have been the Lord's will", they say. Those who pray with faith are only satisfied when they have received the answer they expect, that they want. And they will keep on praying and believing until that specific prayer receives its specific answer. Nothing less will do.

That does not mean that we can dictate to God *how* He is to answer, or even *when* the answer is to come. It does mean that, as His new covenant children, we can afford to be specific and clear about what we ask, believing that we have already received the answer, knowing our Father *will* do it for us as He has promised. How He does it and when is up to Him. The promise Jesus gives is: "It will be yours."

The Way to Ask

Here is a simple way to pray the prayer of faith, as Jesus teaches in Mark 11: 22–24.

1. *Set* your mind on God. Remember His love for you; that you are His child. Spend some time in praise – giving yourself to Him in worship.

2. *Ask* yourself the question: "What do I believe God will do in answer to my prayer?"

3. *If* you have any doubts that He will meet the need, confess them and ask Him to give you the faith of Jesus, the tiny seed that when planted will surely bring the harvest.

4. *Bring* to the Lord anything else that needs to be put right with Him, especially any sin that needs to be forgiven.

5. *Forgive* anybody who has wronged or hurt you.

6. *Thank* the Lord for His forgiveness.

7. *Look* at your mountain – the problem or need that is before you. Don't spend time anxiously thinking about it; rather—

8. *Tell* it to move! It often helps to picture in your mind

the problem being resolved. See it happening with the eyes of faith.

9. *Look* again to the Lord and thank Him that what you are seeing with the eyes of faith, He will do. He will move the mountain.

10. *Praise* Him for His faithfulness, in fulfilling His promise.

11. *Maintain* that attitude of praise and thanksgiving every day until you see the answer to your prayer. Take the shield of faith to parry all the negative thoughts, words and attitudes, and the lying accusations of Satan. (Following chapters will help to show you how to do this.)

12. Continue to give to the Lord and know that He will give to you.

The above is only a guide – not a formula. The only way to learn to pray with faith is by doing it.

Your words of faith: "WHATEVER YOU ASK IN PRAYER, BELIEVE THAT YOU HAVE RECEIVED IT, AND IT WILL BE YOURS."

18

It Will be Yours

THEREFORE I TELL you, whatever you ask in prayer, believe that you have received it, *and it will be yours* (Mark 11: 24).

Jesus does not say that if you 'feel' anything it will be yours. He doesn't say, if you 'experience' anything it will be yours. He doesn't say, if your healing happens *instantly* it will be yours.

He says: "Believe that you have received it, and IT WILL BE YOURS."

Often the testing time for your faith will not be the time of prayer, the moment you ask, but your attitude afterwards.

Praying with faith is knowing that God is your faithful loving Father, who has bound Himself to you under the covenant, to keep all His words of promise. Therefore whatever you ask in the name of Jesus, He will do for you. You continue to pray believing that you have received it, knowing that "it will be yours." You cannot dictate to God how He will do it or when He will do it. But YOU KNOW THAT HE WILL DO IT.

'Rockets' and 'Tortoises'

When talking with our children about God answering prayers, we talk about 'rockets' and 'tortoises'. Some answers come zooming home fast like a rocket, right on targe⁴. We like those answers; fast, immediate. If we had our way, every prayer would have a 'rocket' answer!

In practice, other answers seem to come so slowly, creeping towards us like tortoises, plodding along step by step. But the answer is coming, It is on its way. It will arrive in due course, in God's time. So we keep believing. We continue to pray with thanksgiving that the answer *is* on the way, the healing, the guidance, or whatever it may be.

"It will be yours"; "it will be given you"; "it will be done for you"; these are the words of Jesus.

> No distrust made him (Abraham) waver concerning the promise of God, but he grew strong in his faith as he gave glory to God, fully convinced that God was able to do what he had promised (Rom. 4: 20–21).

But it is so easy to give up before the 'tortoise' arrives. And when you stop believing, the tortoise stops moving towards you. Its head shoots back into its shell! There the answer to your prayer remains, suspended somewhere between heaven and you. And when it doesn't arrive, it is so easy to blame God for not answering. "Why, Lord, why?"

> Therefore, do not throw away your confidence, which has a great reward. For you have need of endurance, so that you may do the will of God and receive what is promised (Heb. 10: 35–36).

God wants you not only to ask with faith, believing that you have received it, but also to patiently endure until you see the fulfilment of the promise, until the answer arrives.

> Let us draw near with a true heart in full assurance of faith ... let us hold fast the confession of our hope without wavering, for he who promised is faithful (Heb. 10: 22–23).

Don't Believe the Doubts

While waiting for the arrival of the answer, there will be many temptations to doubt. There have been occasions when I have started to believe God, but at some time during the waiting period I have begun to believe the doubts instead. The tortoise goes into its shell! It stops moving until I begin to believe again!

It is easier to believe the circumstances before your eyes, rather than the promise that God gives you, to meet the need and remedy the problem. Things may appear to get very much worse, before they get better. That is a real test of faith whether to believe the words of God, or one's own experience. The confrontation between 'faith' and experience.

When people give up and stop looking to God for the answer to the problem, it is often an indication that they did not truly believe in the first place. They did not believe that they had received it. God wants to use the time of waiting to build our trust and confidence in His faithfulness. All too often He has to show us that we do not have the faith that He wants to see in us.

Persist in Prayer

Some people interpret the phrase "believe that you have received it", by saying that you should only pray for a situation once, believe it is done and then forget it. If healing is being sought, you should only ask for ministry once. The repetition of the prayer or request for the laying on of hands, is an indication of a lack of faith, that the individual does not really believe. "If you believe that you have received it," some people argue, "how can you ask again? How can you ask to receive what you believe you have already received?"

It is certainly true that much repetitive prayer demonstrates a lack of faith. For example if I need healing I could say: "Lord, please heal me." Tomorrow I could repeat the same prayer, and the day after, and the day after that. In a month's time I could still be praying the same prayer: "Lord, please heal me."

I am obviously persisting in prayer, but I am not persisting in praying with faith. In which case I could still be praying the same words in a year's time and wondering why God wasn't answering!

If I had faith for my healing, my prayer would be different: "Lord, please heal me, according to the promise of your Word and I thank you for your faithful answer." After that it would be a question of continuing in thanksgiving: "Thank you, Lord, for my healing." And I would need to persist in that faithful attitude until the healing was manifested in my life. That would mean continuing in thanksgiving through all the times when assailed by doubts, when the circumstances seemed unchanged or when it appeared that the prayer had made no difference. Persevering in thanksgiving because my Lord said: "Believe that you have received it, and *it will be yours.*"

This is not, of course, a matter of words, but of believing in your heart, the words that you speak.

The same principle applies to seeking ministry for a specific need. I have known many people to have been healed over a prolonged period of time, having received the laying on of hands on several occasions. But the ministry needs to be in a spirit of thanksgiving that the original request for healing is being answered, and the healing received. It is happening!

Perhaps on the first occasion, the person did not have much confidence that God would heal. But as the healing begins, so the faith and expectancy grows. Subsequent times of ministry can therefore be more fruitful.

To suggest that we should pray only once and then forget the matter, closes the possibility for such answers and is not consistent with Jesus' teaching on persisting in prayer.

"And he told them a parable to the effect that they ought always to pray and not lose heart" (Luke 18: 1).

Jesus' words: "Ask, and it will be given you", can be literally translated, "keep on asking and it will be given you." And in the next verse, "everyone who keeps on asking receives."

So we are told to persist in our praying, which is another way of saying that we are to persist in our believing, until the answer arrives. We do not lose heart if the outward circumstances do not change immediately. Paul says:

> Have no anxiety about anything, but in everything by prayer and supplication with thanksgiving let your requests be made known to God (Phil. 4: 6).

Mistaken Attitude

Some people have been hurt by a mistaken interpretation of Jesus's words: "believe that you have received it, and it will be yours" – particularly in the realm of healing. There are those who assert: "As soon as you have prayed, you are healed! Ignore all the symptoms and pain, and exercise your faith!"

Sometimes people are advised to discharge themselves from hospital, to stop all medical treatment, get out of their sick-beds and behave as if they were healed. It is not difficult to imagine the disastrous consequences that can result from such advice.

The promise is: "it WILL be yours". Jesus does not say that it will be yours *immediately*. He does not tell us to perform acts of foolhardy bravado to try to prove that we believe and that we are trusting Him. In fact, if anything, such acts indicate a lack of faith. It seems that people who adopt such an approach are not prepared to trust God to honour His promise in the way that He decides, at the time that He knows is best.

Beware of those who encourage such acts of so-called

'faith'! The problem is accentuated by the authority that they claim. "The Lord says you are to do this," they say. "God is telling me that you are to discharge yourself from hospital."

And if the sick person refuses, or obeys but has to take to his bed again, he is merely told: "You don't have the faith, brother!"

As Christians, we are to forgive such unloving spiritual blundering. It is not easy always to do so. It doesn't seem to occur to such people that, if they are involved in the situation, their own faith is just as much at stake. A pertinent question can be asked of them: "Do you have the faith and authority to address the mountain and see it moved?"

No Spiritual Blackmail

Praying with faith is not dictating to God; it is trusting Him to keep His word, knowing in your heart that He will. Dispensing with medical attention does not impress God. Often that is the channel that He will use to bring healing into a person's life.

A young woman wanted her eyes to be healed. She prayed, and then as an 'act of faith' she broke her glasses and threw them away. She spent several weeks with impaired eyesight before having to obtain a new pair of spectacles.

The breaking of the glasses proved nothing. If you believe the promise, you know God is going to heal regardless of how many pairs you have! In this particular case it was the action of a new Christian; so it is easy to understand her making such a mistake. The time to throw away your glasses or your crutches is when the Lord has healed you, and your body manifests the evidence of that healing. God is not honoured by a well-meaning Christian hobbling into his doctor's surgery, saying, "The Lord has healed my foot. By faith I believe it."

Our faith needs to be in His words of promise, not in gestures of spiritual bravado. Before Peter climbed out of the boat, when Jesus was standing on the water, he waited until he heard for himself the command: "Come". His faith was in response to the words of Jesus.

Anyone who jumps out of the boat before he personally hears the Lord telling him to, can expect to sink.

It is fine to say, "By faith I believe it." Keep on saying it. But wait until you have seen the evidence of the answer in your body before you testify about your healing.

"*All Prayer is with Faith*"

On the other hand, there is much teaching on prayer and healing that assures people that whatever they do is an expression of faith. The very fact that people pray it is claimed, demonstrates 'faith'. There is some truth in this; but because a person prays does not mean he has the 'mustard seed' faith that Jesus speaks of, knowing that the prayer seed will certainly produce the required harvest.

It is easier to pray than to believe! It is possible to ask, but without the faith that Jesus speaks of.

"*I Really Believe*"

Many people come for prayer, the laying on of hands or anointing and really 'believe' that God is going to heal them. But they go away disappointed because they feel that "nothing has happened". It is then assumed that God must have some other purpose, that perhaps it is not His will to heal in that situation. Yet that would be a denial of Jesus' prayer promises: "*whatever* you ask . . ."

We are confronted again, with two different interpretations of 'faith': what Christians usually mean by this word, and what Jesus means by it.

The person coming for a time of ministry is not going to leave disappointed if He believes that He has already received. He will go away rejoicing knowing the faithfulness of God and that it will be done. He has asked in faith and God will answer that faith. Even if at the time there is no outward evidence of healing.

The problem for him may be that the healing hasn't happened instantly. Jesus does not promise that it will. He says that the answer to the prayer 'will be yours'.

Faith says: "I BELIEVE."

Doubt, expressed in disappointment says: "I BELIEVED!"

Faith is a continuous attitude of believing until the answer is seen.

In recent years I have prayed with countless people to be healed. Many, at the time of prayer, would have said that they did not experience or feel anything happening. And yet within a few days they are testifying to their healing. Only this week I received a letter telling of two people with whom I prayed recently, both with back troubles. I had been teaching about the prayer of faith, and the need to go on believing until the answer was received.

Apparently when we prayed on the Sunday evening, neither person noticed any significant change in their physical condition. By the following Wednesday, both had received their healing. On the Sunday, they could have said that the prayer hadn't worked, although they had believed. They could have given in to their disappointment and adopted the attitude: "We'll try another time, somewhere else."

Instead, they had heard the promises of Jesus and they held on to them until the healing was received. Two or three days does not seem very long to wait for the answer to arrive – unless you are the one who has the bad back! There can be a lot of temptation to doubt in three days, many opportunities to give up believing and give way to disappointment.

But if you believe that you have received it your only

disappointment will be that the healing did not come like a 'rocket'. You will still be rejoicing and praising God because you know it will be yours.

Not 'Feelings'

Some people don't get as far as the time of waiting. They only believe in 'rockets'. This can be a danger, particularly when seeking ministry for healing. If, when they pray, they do not 'feel' or 'experience' anything, they often doubt whether God is honouring His promise. In reality, their trust can be in the 'feeling' or the 'experience' rather than in the words of God: "it will be yours". In which case their faith is built on sand, and they are destined for many disappointments until they build on rock.

During times of ministry, the Lord sends many 'rocket' answers. We have to learn to be just as thankful for the 'tortoises'. God's wisdom is infinitely greater than ours; He knows best, when and how we are to receive the answer. And His Spirit, alive within us, will lead us faithfully to that point of receiving as we continue to believe the words of Jesus that He declares to us.

Failure is Forgiven

I have had to look back over my Christian life and ask God to forgive all the times when I gave in to the doubts and believed them over and above His promises. How wonderful it is that every time we confess our failure, God wipes the slate clean! He forgives completely. He gives a new start. He doesn't condemn us for the past, but gives us a new opportunity to believe for the future.

He does not want *you* to feel condemned either. He does not want you to be constantly living under the cloud of your past failures. If He has shown you that there were times when you didn't really believe Him for the answer to a problem, perhaps an important need, bring the failure to Him straight away, and receive His forgiveness. If you began to believe for an answer, but gave up after a while because you believed the circumstances, rather than the promise, ask the Lord to forgive your lack of perseverance. If you have only looked for 'rockets' in the past, pray the prayer of faith now and believe that "it will be yours".

Know that God is concerned about the future; that you can have a new, positive, faith-full attitude towards asking in prayer. As you learn to pray the prayer of faith, you will believe Him and hang on to His promises, even if it is only by your finger-nails – as it will be sometimes!

Your words of faith: "IT WILL BE YOURS." "IT WILL BE GIVEN YOU." "IT WILL BE DONE FOR YOU."

19

In My Name

IF YOU ASK anything IN MY NAME, I will do it (John 14: 14).

By now these words will be familiar to you. In the previous verse Jesus says:

Whatever you ask IN MY NAME, I will do it, that the Father may be glorified in the Son (John 14: 13).

In both, Jesus speaks of asking "in my name", and later He talks of receiving "in my name".

Truly, truly, I say to you, if you ask anything of the Father, he will give it to you IN MY NAME (John 16: 23).

The name of Jesus is more than a title; it implies His whole Person. It is "in the name" of Jesus that the disciples are given power to heal the sick and cast out demons. They are given the authority to do the same works as Jesus did, as if it was He Himself doing them.

"Where two or three are gathered IN MY NAME, there am I in the midst of them" (Matt. 18: 20). The Person of Jesus is present because they come together "in His name".

"Whoever receives one such child IN MY NAME receives ME" (Matt. 18: 5). To receive anyone "in His name" is to receive the Lord Himself, the Person of Jesus.

To pray in the name of Jesus is to bring His Person into the prayer. It is as if Jesus Himself was praying that prayer to His Father. Jesus tells us to "ask in my name". That is the way He wants us to pray.

To bring the person of Jesus into the prayer is to pray with His love, His purpose and His *faith*. If that seems impossible for you, remember that God has given you His Holy Spirit, so that you can be filled with His love, know His purpose and be inspired with His faith!

As you face a situation that requires prayer, you can ask yourself these questions:

1. How would Jesus *love* in this situation?
That is the way I want to love.

2. What would Jesus *do* in this situation?
That is what I want to do.

3. What would Jesus *believe* in this situation?
That is how I want to believe.

As you learn to pray in the name of Jesus, you learn to put yourself in His shoes, so that you approach the problem as He would, knowing that all the resources of heaven are at your disposal. Your Father does not want you to be full of doubt, insecurity and despair. He wants you to pray with the confidence of Jesus, knowing that you are God's child.

Jesus in the Prayer

To pray "in the name of Jesus" means that you bring Him into the prayer. He prays along with you. He approaches the problem with you. You face it together, in His power, with His faith, that mustard-seed faith that moves mountains; with His love. "Abide in me, and I in you." When you pray, you live in Jesus, and he lives in you. Your prayer is a combined operation!

So if you pray "in the name of Jesus", your prayers can have the effectiveness of those of Jesus Himself. We cannot conceive of the Father ignoring any prayer of His own Son. Neither will He ignore any of the prayers of His children

who pray in His name, within the covenant relationship that
He has given them.

Not a Formula

Unfortunately, "in the name of Jesus" has become a
formula that is tacked on to the end of most prayers, to give
them an air of authenticity and so that others present know
when it is time to say, 'Amen'! Prayer does not achieve
significant results when it is reduced to a series of formulae.
It is not the words spoken that are significant, but what is
going on in the heart of the one praying. Is he praying along
with Jesus? Is his prayer expressing the love and concern of
Jesus? Is he believing God to work, as Jesus believes His
Father to work in every situation?

When Jesus prayed, He looked up to heaven expectantly.
He didn't look at the mountain and think it immovable! He
knew the resources that were available to Him and those
same resources are available to *you*. You don't have to feel
defeated before you begin. You have been given the privilege of praying in Jesus' name, of having Him in your
prayer. Use that great privilege.

Remember that He promises you that, "if you ask anything in my name, I will do it"!

If Jesus is in the prayer with you, He will make sure that
the promises are fulfilled, that "it will be yours". Together
you will look to the Father so that, "if you ask anything of
the Father, he will give it to you in my name." The Father
will give to you, as He gives to Jesus, because you are at one
with Him in your prayer.

What possibilities lie before you, as you pray "in the
name of Jesus", realising that He is praying with you!

**Your words of faith: "WHATEVER YOU ASK IN MY
NAME, I WILL DO IT."**

20

Anything You Want

TRULY, TRULY, I say to you, if you ask *anything* of the Father, he will give it to you in my name. Hitherto you have asked nothing in my name; ask, and you will receive, that your joy may be full (John 16: 23–24).

ANYTHING! "Truly, truly, I say to you ..." means, "I say this with great emphasis". The disciples were to take particular note of what Jesus was to say.

During the course of His ministry, they had become used to His physical presence with them, speaking His Father's words and doing His works. They would have prayed to God as 'Father', as Jesus had taught them. But they had never asked God to do anything as if it was Jesus Himself asking. They had never prayed "in the name of Jesus".

With the crucifixion imminent, He had given them the promise that the Holy Spirit would soon come to live in them: "your hearts will rejoice, and no one will take your joy from you" (John 16: 22). Jesus will then be alive in them to pray in them, and to perform His Father's works through them:

Truly, truly, I say to you, he who believes in me will also do the works that I do; and greater works than these will he do, because I go to the Father (John 14: 12).

That is a promise for "he who believes in me"; any one who puts his faith in Jesus. For those who truly pray "in the name of Jesus" pray with Him, with the limitless resources of His power. During the days of His earthly ministry, Jesus was limited like all humans, by time and space. Now that He reigns in glory with the Father, He has to suffer no such limitations. He is in us and with us as we pray in His name, and yet Presence and power can be directed anywhere at any time, through believing prayer. That is one of the reasons why Jesus did not want the disciples to be sad about His imminent death; it would open up untold possibilities for the future.

Jesus told them to pray "in my name", so that as His continuing Body here on earth, the Father could go on giving to them as He had been giving to Him during the days of His humanity.

Father or Son

You can pray to either the Father or the Son. Jesus said: "I and the Father are one" (John 10: 30).

> Whatever you ask in my name, *I will do it*.
> If you ask anything in my name, *I will do it*.

Jesus is making it clear that He wants to *do* things *for* His followers, even after the crucifixion and resurrection. At the same time, He tells them to pray to His Father:

> Whatever you ask the Father in my name, *he may give it to you*.
> If you ask anything of the Father, *he will give it to you* in my name.

The Father wants to give to His children, as He has given to His Son, during the days of His humanity.

Whether you pray to the Father or the Son, what matters is that you pray in the name of Jesus, with His faith, knowing the willingness of your covenant God to give to you and to work for you; that your prayer is filled with the presence of Jesus, with His love, life and power.

Two Motives

Jesus says that He will do anything we ask Him "in His name", "that the Father may be glorified in the Son". That is His purpose; to glorify His Father. That is also our purpose as Christians, to bear fruit for His glory.

He says that the Father will give us anything we ask in Jesus' name, "that your joy may be full". A loving Father is blessed by giving to His children, and seeing their joy in receiving.

To say that God wants to bless His children, is to realise that He wants them to be happy, for their "joy to be full".

He wants to give to *you.*

Whatever You Want

Jesus is not afraid to tell us to pray for "whatever you will", anything you want, because He knows that the Holy Spirit is going to stir right desires in the new hearts that God has given His new covenant children. If you or someone else is sick or in some other need, it is instinctive for you, as a Christian, to pray for that person. The Spirit within you urges you to pray.

Your mind may tell you something else. You may think, "It is useless. It is pointless. No good will come of my prayer." But the Spirit will say "Pray!" And Jesus living within you will want you to pray, with His faith, in His name, believing that you have received it.

Believing God to meet needs is one thing, but does He really mean we can ask for *anything* that we want? Yes, He does.

It has often delighted me that God has answered prayers

for unnecessary, even trivial things that could hardly be described as necessities. But then any loving Father wants to provide His children with more than the bare necessities of life. And our heavenly Father loves supremely, more abundantly than any human father. He is concerned about every area of our lives, even the seemingly insignificant ones. He will not allow us to abuse His generosity; but He doesn't want us to waste it either!

James says: "You do not have, because you do not ask" (James 4: 2). God wants to teach you to trust Him in all the small details, as well as the great needs. To be looking to Him to "do for you" and to "give to you", anything that you ask in the name of Jesus.

And remember that not only is He glorified in giving to His new covenant children, but that He also wants "your joy to be full". He delights in giving, He delights in seeing the faith that believers give to Him, and He delights in the joy of His children as they receive.

Asking Amiss

"How can I be sure that what I am praying for is right in the eyes of God?" To pray according to God's will is rightly a great concern for Christians. Some are quick to quote James's words:

> You ask and do not receive, because you ask wrongly, to spend it on your passions. Unfaithful creatures! (James 4: 3–4).

Jesus did not pray to indulge His passions! You will not be able to pray "in the name of Jesus" to indulge yours either. You cannot pray with Jesus, or be confident that He is praying with you, for anything that you know is contrary to His purpose. It is possible to pray for wrong things with selfish motives. But you cannot pray such things with the faith of Jesus. The Holy Spirit within you will not inspire such faith to pray for anything opposed to the Father's will. Neither is Jesus going to be praying with you in that prayer. And you can be sure that the Father is not likely to give you what is opposed to His loving purpose for you.

There are many things that your 'flesh' may tell you that you would like to have right now. You do not pray the prayer of faith for them because you know all too well that you would only be indulging your passions, and not praying as Jesus would.

However, most of your asking prayer will be for genuine needs, in your own life and in the lives of others. You need not hesitate in approaching those needs as Jesus would, with love and compassion, with power and with faith. You need not be tentative in your thinking or in your praying. Jesus never was.

Confront that need before you now. Tell the mountain to move and ask Jesus to work for you in that situation; ask the Father to give whatever is necessary. And remember:

God *wants* you to ask.

He *wants* you to believe that you have it.

He *wants* you to pray "in the name of Jesus".

He *wants* to be glorified in giving to you.

He *wants* your joy to be full.

He *wants* you to have a fruitful prayer life.

Your words of faith: "ASK, AND YOU WILL RECEIVE, THAT YOUR JOY MAY BE FULL."

21

Every Need

FEAR IS THE opposite of faith. When you are afraid, you are not trusting God.

We all experience fear and anxiety during the course of our daily lives; fears about work, children, finance, the future and so on.

God gives us a very simple command: "Fear not" – a command that is repeated hundreds of times in the Bible. This was a phrase often on the lips of Jesus. He assured his hearers that His Father knew their needs, and wanted to meet them. So there was no necessity to be fearful or anxious.

> In praying do not heap up empty phrases as the Gentiles do; for they think they will be heard for their many words. Do not be like them, for *your Father knows what you need before you ask him* (Matt. 6: 7–8).

God is looking for the faith in your asking that will release the answers to those needs into your life.

> Therefore I tell you, do not be anxious about your life, what you shall eat or what you shall drink, nor about your body, what you shall put on (Matt 6: 25).

"Your heavenly Father feeds the birds", Jesus goes on to say. Trust Him to feed you, to meet your needs. Besides, "Which of you by being anxious can add one cubit to his span of life?" (v. 27). What good will all your worrying do you? None. Instead, have faith in the promises of your Father.

If God so clothes the grass of the field, which today is alive and tomorrow is thrown into the oven, will he not much more clothe you, O men of little faith? Therefore DO NOT BE ANXIOUS, saying, What shall we eat? or What shall we drink? or What shall we wear? For the Gentiles seek all these things; and your heavenly Father knows that you need them all (vv. 30–32).

The 'Gentiles' here are the faithless ones, those who were outside the covenant relationship between God and Israel. You are within the new covenant and so need have no anxiety about anything.

God is YOUR Father. You are His child, a child of the new covenant. All His promises are for *you*. He loves *you*. He cares for *you*. He wants to meet *all your* needs. And He knows about them, even before you ask Him.

The Kingdom First

When you pray, you are not asking God to do something that He doesn't want to do. You are blessing Him by allowing Him to honour your faith and give to you. And so Jesus tells us:

But seek first his kingdom and his righteousness, and all these things shall be yours as well (Matt. 6: 33).

Another great promise, following an important command. Every need in your life will be met if you seek first the kingdom of God and are in a right relationship with Him. This is why you need to give yourself whole-heartedly to the Lord, so that you might be made righteous through the blood of Jesus, brought into a right relationship with Him, knowing Him as 'Father' and being filled with his Holy Spirit. Submitting everything to Him that He might be 'Lord' and 'King' in your life. That He might reign supreme in you. That you might live, not for your own selfish ends, but for Him. To honour Him. To give Him glory.

The Lord's Prayer

If you live for Him, God promises that "all these things will be yours as well". Jesus tells us to pray to:

"Our Father who art in heaven": That is the wonderful privilege of His children; not only to know Him as 'Father', to be in that kind of a relationship with God, but to call upon Him to use all His heavenly resources to meet our needs according to His promises. Remembering, of course, that we are not to demand from God. If we believe His promises, He will give.

That word 'Father' is most precious to a Christian. It speaks of His love, care, concern, of His willingness to give.

"Hallowed be thy name": If you 'know' God, the greatest desire of your heart is to praise Him for all that He is: the great, almighty, holy God, who is *your* Father. There is no greater joy than that of praise, of being lifted before the throne of God in worship and adoration.

All your asking needs to be set within the context of praise. For it is then that your eyes will be fixed, not on the problem, but on the One who is the answer to it. And the more you praise, the greater your awareness of the immensity of God, and the wonder of His love for you.

To praise the name of your God, is to praise Him 'in Person'. That is *your* privilege.

"Thy kingdom come, thy will be done, on earth as it is in heaven": You can only pray these words "from the heart" if you relate them to your own life. You cannot meaningfully pray God's will to be done on earth unless you are prepared to do His will yourself. So you are saying to your Father: "I want you to reign in my life and in the lives of all your

people. I want your will to be done in me and in everybody else."

Jesus wants you to live 'kingdom life' here on earth. That means that you do not approach every situation from a purely human point of view, but realise that all the resources of heaven are available to you. As you pray, believing the promises of your Father, those resources are brought to earth.

It is not only the faith of Jesus that the Father wants to see in His children. He is looking for His love in them, to see His life being lived out in them, expressed in their care for one another and their desire to reach out with their heavenly resources to meet the needs of others.

"Give us this day our daily bread": Again Jesus impresses upon us His wish that we ask our Father to *give* to us. "Daily bread" means that we ask Him for everything that we need to enable us to do His will and to live that kingdom life here on earth.

And Jesus tells us to pray: "Give us *this day.*" Our prayers are not to be those of vague hope that one day in the future we might receive something from God. Rather, our expectancy is to be that God will meet our needs *today*; He will provide for us *today*.

"And forgive us our debts, as we also have forgiven our debtors": Unforgiven sin can so easily prevent us from receiving what our Father wants to give to us. He is always prepared to forgive His children and to restore them to that union with Himself that He enjoys with them.

So often His way is that He will give to us, only when we have given first. This is particularly true of forgiveness. Notice the words Jesus uses: ". . . as we also have forgiven."

You forgive those who wrong you, and God will forgive you for the ways in which you have wronged Him.

At the end of the Lord's prayer, Jesus underlines this point emphatically by saying: "For if you forgive men their trespasses, your heavenly Father also will forgive you; but if you do not forgive men their trespasses, neither will your Father forgive your trespasses" (Matt 6: 14–15).

"*And lead us not into temptation*": God does not want us to disobey His will, to deny His reign in our lives, or to disbelieve His words. Throughout all the times when we are tempted to doubt His promise or give up trusting Him for the answer to our prayers, He is with us. He never gives up on us; He never deserts us: "I will be with you; I will not fail you or forsake you."

Against every temptation to doubt, He wants us to take the shield of faith, and hold on to His words, that our trust and confidence will always be in Him.

"*But deliver us from evil*": It is God's purpose to save us from every manifestation of evil: bodily sickness, mental fear and a doubting spirit. He sent His Son to die on the Cross to make that possible. And He wants the victory of Calvary to be brought in every situation of need in our lives, by believing prayer.

Good Things

> Ask and it shall be given you; seek, and you will find; knock and it will be opened to you. For EVERYONE WHO ASKS RECEIVES, and he who seeks finds, and to him who knocks it will be opened (Matt. 7: 7–8).

It will be . . . It will be . . . It will be . . . It will be . . .
That is the emphatic promise of Jesus.

"Everyone who asks receives." EVERYONE – that includes YOU.

Everyone who asks from the heart, believing the promise that God gives through His Son. And when you ask, remember what kind of a Father you have in heaven:

> Or what man of you, if his son asks him for bread, will give him a stone? Or if he asks for a fish, will give him a

serpent? If you then, who are evil, know how to give good gifts to your children, HOW MUCH MORE WILL YOUR FATHER WHO IS IN HEAVEN GIVE GOOD THINGS TO THOSE WHO ASK HIM! (Matt. 7: 9–11).

That is your Father's good pleasure: to give you good things. He sent His Son to deliver you from all that is evil so that in His Fatherly love He may give you that abundance of life, prosperity and healing, which is His purpose for you.

The thief comes only to steal and kill and destroy; I came that they may have life, and have it abundantly (John 10: 10)

Satan is 'the thief'. He sets out to steal from you. He wants to take away your joy and fill your life with worry and anxiety. He wants to take the love for others out of your life and fill you with fear and suspicion and even hate. He wants to destroy your faith in God and fill you with unbelief. He is dedicated to destroying your health of body, mind and spirit. He wants to disturb your peace, give sickness and pain to your body.

And God does not want you to bow before any of these works of Satan and submit to them. If he is given the opportunity the enemy will kill you physically and he will destroy your faith. His ultimate joy would be to kill you spiritually, so that you do not enjoy that eternal life with your Father, that is your inheritance as His child.

Victory

But Jesus came to bring life, not death; to bring victory, not defeat; to bring healing, not sickness; to do you good, not evil. It is His Father's will and purpose to "give good things to those who ask him".

He sent His Son to die on the Cross to make the defeat of Satan and all His works absolute, total. The victory is there waiting for you to enter into through faith.

You do not have to ask if God wants any of these evil things in your life. Imperfect human fathers know how to give good gifts to their children. How much more will your Father, who is perfect love and perfect goodness, want to do good things in your life and set you free from every manifestation of evil. It cost Him the life of His dear Son to make that possible. And he doesn't want that cost wasted.

And He doesn't want you to believe in anything less than God's perfect wholeness for you; health of body, soul and spirit. He wants to meet every need of whatever nature.

> Beloved, I pray that you may prosper in every way and that you may be in health; I know that it is well with your soul (3 John 2).

Your words of faith: "YOUR FATHER KNOWS WHAT YOU NEED BEFORE YOU ASK HIM."

22

The Healing Lord

JESUS WAS NOT one to preach one thing and practise another. In the previous chapter we looked at some of the things He said during the Sermon on the Mount.

> "Your Father knows what you need before you ask him."
> "Do not be anxious about your life . . ."
> "Seek first his kingdom and his righteousness, and all these things will be yours as well."
> "Give us this day our daily bread."
> "Ask and it will be given you."
> "Everyone who asks receives."

How did Jesus put these words into operation in His own ministry? We will follow the events recorded in Matthew's Gospel, after the Sermon on the Mount. Chapter eight opens with the healing of a leper.

A Leper

"Lord, if you will, you can make me clean" (Matt. 8: 2), the leper says to Jesus. Many people approach healing today with a similar diffidence. They ask to be healed, but add "if it be your will" at the end of their prayer. The 'if' must go. Jesus answered the leper simply "I want to" (or "I am willing to" or "I will"). It is His purpose to give abundant life, not see us die from crippling and evil diseases.

You cannot pray the prayer of faith, looking to God with

confidence and expectancy, when there is an 'if' to your prayer. Ask "in my name," said Jesus, "as if I was praying the prayer myself, with my faith, my expectancy, with my life and power and Presence." Jesus never turned anyone away who came to Him. And He did not use any 'ifs' when He prayed for people to be healed.

> And he stretched out his hand and touched him, saying "I will; be clean." And immediately his leprosy was cleansed (v. 3).

Jesus heals the leper with a touch and a word of authority: "Be clean". Here we see the Son speaking the words His Father gives Him to speak, and doing the works He saw His Father doing. Loving. Caring. Healing. Restoring. Meeting with the leper at his point of need. Jesus didn't preach Him a sermon. He healed him!

You need not doubt that God, your loving Father, desires to heal you. Either you have to say: "God wants me to have this sickness", or you have to believe "God does not want me to have this sickness". If you think He wants you to have it then you have no right to go to a doctor, or try to lessen the pain, or even to pray about it. To do any of these things would be to go against what you say is God's will for you.

This seems clearly ridiculous! He is certainly not a loving Father who wants to "give good things" to His children, if you think His best purpose for you is sickness and pain.

So what is the alternative? He wants to heal! In which case you have every right to pray; to ask, believing His promise; to seek the good offices of the medical profession. To believe God, not only to alleviate the pain, but remove the disease, whether it is physical, mental or emotional; and to give you the healing you seek in the way He chooses.

The Centurion

As Jesus entered Capernaum, He was approached by a Roman centurion, who said "Lord, my servant is lying paralysed at home, in terrible distress" (Matt. 8: 6). Did Jesus say: "Well leave him alone; it is my Father's will that he is sick and is suffering so terribly?" Of course not! Jesus said: "I will come and heal him" (v. 7).

Both the leper and the centurion CAME to Jesus with their need. It is made clear in the gospels that Jesus met the needs of ALL who CAME to Him. He did not go to every sick person in every city, town and village that He visited in order to heal them.

Occasionally Jesus took the initiative, as, for example, with the man by the pool of Bethesda. But the general principle is that all who came, or were brought, were healed.

If you need healing, it is for you to 'come' to Jesus, rather than sit back and wait for Him to come to you. To come to Him with faith, believing "that you have received it" and being sure of His promise to you: "and it will be yours".

The centurion came on behalf of His servant; then Jesus offers to come and heal the man. This is the Lord's way: "You come to me FIRST and then I will come to you."

The Roman soldier surprises Jesus by saying to Him:

"Lord, I am not worthy to have you come under my roof, but only say the word and my servant will be healed. For I am a man under authority, with soldiers under me and I say to one, 'Go', and he goes, and to another 'Come', and he comes, and to my slave. 'Do this', and he does it." When Jesus heard him, he marvelled ... (Matt. 8–10).

Men often marvelled at the things Jesus said; here Jesus marvels at the words the centurion speaks. "Truly, I say to you, not even in Israel have I found such FAITH" (v. 10).

This Gentile, this Roman soldier of the occupation forces, comes to Him calling Him 'Lord'. And when Jesus offers to come and heal his servant, the man says: "That won't be necessary; you only have to give the order and it will be done. I know that because I have to obey orders, and give them. And when I give an order I expect instant obedience."

Jesus says that the centurion's words and attitude demonstrated more FAITH than He had found in Israel – even among His own disciples! What is so remarkable about the centurion? He understood the authority of Jesus.

Jesus is the Son of God; nothing is impossible for Him. He only has to speak the word, or give the order, and it is done. When Jesus speaks, Almighty God speaks. When Jesus acts, His heavenly Father is at work.

Do you understand the authority and power of the One whom you call: 'Lord'? If so, you know that He only has to speak His word to your heart and you will be healed. The Holy Spirit only has to take the words of Jesus and declare them to you, and the promise will be fulfilled.

Faith, as Jesus understands it, is believing "that you have received it". And He saw that quality of faith in the Roman soldier. Jesus links directly this faith with the healing that follows. He speaks the word of authority. He gives His order. "Go; be it done for you *as you have believed*" (Matt. 8: 13). Ask with faith – and it WILL be done.

Peter's Mother-in-law

Next, Jesus entered Peter's house, where the disciple's mother-in-law was "lying sick with a fever. He touched her hand, and the fever left her, and she rose and served him". What better motive could there be for receiving healing from Jesus, than rising to serve the Lord?

Jesus healed the centurion's servant with a word: Peter's mother-in-law with a touch; the leper with a word and a touch.

Touch can be so important in ministering to those who need healing. To sit and hold the hand of a sick person can be a great comfort to them, even if no words are spoken. The physical contact can convey love and concern.

The Laying on of Hands

When we minister to others "in the name of Jesus", it is as if the Lord Himself is making the physical contact. When we lay hands on one another, He is using a pair of ordinary human hands, but it can be His touch, if that is what we believe. So we should expect much more than human love and concern to be expressed in a deliberate laying on of hands in the name of Jesus. We can expect nothing less than the healing power of the Lord to be conveyed to the one who is receiving ministry.

That faith and expectation ideally needs to be in both the patient and those ministering to him. All concerned should have adequate preparation before such a time of ministry. Jesus heals those who 'come' to Him and so, when possible, the one seeking healing should be encouraged to come, offering his life afresh and whole-heartedly to God (see Chapter 8). And those who are ministering should be similarly prepared.

Laying hands on people without any result is not glorifying to the Lord, or helpful to the sick person. Whenever a person comes GIVING himself, the Lord responds by GIVING Himself. When people are only interested in receiving from Him, then the results can be disappointing. When they come without faith, they are unpredictable.

So during the time of preparation before personal ministry it is good for both patient and those praying with him, to 'receive' the promises that God gives in His word concerning answered prayer and healing. (See Chapter 11).

Not Always Instant

We pray according to the promises of Jesus. He does *not* promise instant answers to all our prayers. He does say: "it will be done for you." "It will be given you." "It will be yours." *It will be.*

Sometimes there will be instant healing; at other times a measure of improvement will be seen immediately in the patient. In some, there will be no discernible improvement in the condition, at the time. This is when it is so easy to believe your doubts, rather than the promises of Jesus. "Nothing has happened." "It hasn't worked." "God doesn't want to heal me."

"Believe that you have received it, and it will be yours," Jesus says. Go on believing until you see the answer, the promise fulfilled. Don't give up! Or be tempted to believe your doubts. Don't be concerned if you have not experienced or felt anything.

Why was nearly everyone who came to Jesus healed instantly, and yet that is obviously not the case at healing services today?

At healing services Jesus is ministering His healing power, but imperfect channels, with imperfect faith exercise less than the total authority of Jesus. Obviously, there are some who come looking to the man ministering and not to the Lord: so that can lead to disappointment. There will be others who are hoping for the best, and who do not believe that they have received what they asked for. There are others who come wanting only to receive and not to give to the Lord; they are not seeking first the kingdom of God.

There can be many imponderables; but the promises of Jesus are clear, that, if we believe (in the way that He teaches) then *whatever* we ask will be given to us. In His way. And in His time.

Much distress can be caused when people are taught that the healing must happen instantly, or it will not happen at all. That is not a statement of faith. It is believing our experiences (or lack of them) rather than the promises of Jesus.

When you come to the Lord, either in prayer or in prayer coupled with the laying on of hands, you can come with faith, believing that God is going to heal, and after the prayer, believing that He has. And you need to maintain that faith until the evidence of that healing is plain, rather than be disappointed because God has not acted in the *way* you wanted, *when* you wanted.

"It will be", Jesus promises.

Praise God for the 'rocket' answers! Praise Him for the 'tortoises'; Praise Him for the faith to believe the promises!

Your words of faith: "GO; BE IT DONE FOR YOU AS YOU HAVE BELIEVED."

23

The Healing Cross

THAT EVENING THEY brought to him many who were
possessed with demons; and he cast out the spirits with
a word, and *healed all who were sick* (Matt. 8: 16).

This is one of the many statements that occur throughout
the gospel accounts which show us the outworking of Jesus'
promise: "For every one who asks receives." He "casts out"
the evil spirits "with a word" of command and authority;
and He healed all who were sick, all who were "brought to
him".

The following verse is of paramount importance in understanding why healing played such a significant part in Jesus'
ministry, why He healed all who came or were brought to
Him, and why He will still heal today when we come to Him.

This was to fulfil what was spoken by the prophet
Isaiah, "HE TOOK OUR INFIRMITIES AND
BORE OUR DISEASES" (Matt. 8: 17).

To understand the healing of Jesus we have to come back
to the Cross. In that remarkable prophecy of the Crucifixion
in Isaiah, Chapter 53, we read:

Surely he has borne our griefs (sicknesses)
and carried our sorrows (pains);
yet we esteemed him stricken,
smitten by God, and afflicted.
But he was wounded for our transgressions,
he was bruised for our iniquities;
upon him was the chastisement

that made us whole,
and with his stripes we are healed (Isa. 53: 4–5).

These words were written hundreds of years before the Cross. We look at them hundreds of years after the crucifixion. When they were first spoken they looked forward to what would happen; as we read them, we look back at what has already taken place.

Griefs and Sorrows

Jesus *has borne our griefs and carried our sorrows*. He has taken them to the Cross and crucified them with Him so that all who come to Him can be set free from them.

Many people hold on to their grief, particularly when a very close relative has died. It is natural to grieve; but grief is negative and even self-destructive. It is really a form of self-pity. As Christians, we believe that God's children are liberated at the time of physical death, to enjoy His eternal glory. Resurrection is a time for rejoicing, not mourning. Of course, it is natural for those who loved that person to feel the loss deeply. However, God does not want that loss to cloud the rest of their lives and destroy them with self-pity.

At a meeting in New Zealand, I had been talking about God purchasing us for Himself with the blood of the Cross. Everything that we are and have is His.

In the congregation was a woman whose young grandson had been tragically killed about six weeks previously. This boy was the "apple of her eye". She doted on him and so felt the loss greatly. She was a Christian, but no longer knew what to believe. Grief can so easily shatter faith.

As she listened that day, she realised that she had been holding on to that boy, believing him to be her own. She knew that she had to give him to God, to acknowledge that he was His child. And when it came to the time of ministry, she came forward bringing her grief to the Cross.

On the following day she gave a brief, but deeply moving testimony. She said that previously she was unable to mention the boy's name without breaking down in tears. Yet now as she spoke she looked radiant. She knew that the boy was with the Lord, but more than that, Jesus had "borne her grief" on the Cross and had filled her anew with the joy of His Spirit.

That is our God, the God of love, meeting His children right in the middle of their needs.

Our Sicknesses and Pains

Jesus has borne our sicknesses and carried our pains to the Cross. The Hebrew words used can be translated either 'grief' or 'sickness', and 'sorrow' or 'pain'. Grief and sorrow are mental anguish; sickness and pain are physical suffering. The truth is that Jesus has taken upon Himself both the mental and physical suffering of men, so that, through the Cross, they may be healed of both.

Many people look upon the Cross as a time of victory for the enemies of Jesus. They think of the pitiful sight of the Son of God being crucified: "yet we esteemed him stricken, smitten by God, afflicted." There is no question that His Father led Him deliberately to the Cross, because He was prepared to pay the price with His precious life for our full healing, wholeness and salvation; the healing that He wants in our bodies, minds, spirits, emotions, relationships, problems, and needs.

Jesus was "smitten by God" that we might be healed. That healing is already accomplished! Matthew renders Isaiah 53 verse 4: "He took our infirmities and bore our diseases." As He hung on the Cross Jesus said: "It is accomplished", or "It is finished". It is done. All that is needed for the healing of God's people. Every manifestation of evil was defeated and Jesus' victory made available to

God's children. The resurrection of Jesus is the evidence of that victory. Even death has been defeated.

Our Sin

He was wounded for our transgressions, he was bruised for our iniquities. It is more commonly understood that the sins of men are forgiven because of the finished, accomplished work of the crucifixion. When we enter into fellowship with our heavenly Father, we do so through the Cross; we come to the Lord, confessing our sins and knowing that He is faithful and just to forgive us.

Because of the sacrifice of Jesus, God's forgiveness awaits those who come to Him. When a sinner turns to God, Jesus does not have to die all over again so that he might be accepted and forgiven. His salvation has already been accomplished and awaits that act of turning, or repentance.

So it is with all our other healing needs, which are all part of the salvation that God makes available to us. We come to the Cross, to the place where our grief and sorrow, our sickness and pain, as well as our sins, have been defeated by Jesus.

Those who proclaim forgiveness without preaching healing, are only teaching a partial Cross, an incomplete Gospel. There would be much more evidence of healing in the lives of God's children if they were to BELIEVE as readily in healing through the Cross, as they do in forgiveness. The Lord's forgiveness is taught from infancy in most Christian homes; His healing is sometimes never taught at all!

There are some who claim that the forgiveness is for now, and the healing is in resurrection, in life after death. That plainly will not do. If the forgiveness of the Cross is for NOW, then so is the healing of grief, sorrow, pain, sickness, infirmities and diseases! The rest of verse 5 is the very confirmation of this.

Being Made Whole

> Upon him was the chastisement that made us whole, and with his stripes we are healed (Isa. 53: 5).

The chastisement of Jesus "MADE US WHOLE". Not, "will make us whole after death": but "MADE us whole". 'Whole' means being complete and made perfect in every way, as whole people: healing of body, of the soul, of the mind, of fear and anxiety and doubt; healing of relationships and marriages, of attitudes and problems. Everything. A healing already accomplished and waiting for those who come to Jesus, giving themselves to Him and believing Him.

For "with His stripes WE ARE HEALED". Not, "we will be after death"; "WE ARE HEALED." God gives His Son to the world to heal the world, to heal even the nations.

During this life on earth, we will only appropriate partially this fullness of life that is ours. That is why we do not need to fear physical death. For the Christian, that is a release into the total healing of Jesus.

In the diagram opposite, the oval shape represents the life of a child of God and the solid line, the ideal time for physical death. God's perfect purpose is for us to manifest *now* the wholeness of body, soul and spirit that is available through the Cross of Christ.

However, none of us does manifest the life of Jesus perfectly. Physical death occurs before that, represented by the dotted line. Obviously the Lord wants that dotted line to occur near the solid line, so that as much as possible of the wholeness He desires for us, is manifested during this life on earth. It is right, therefore, to come to the Lord with our healing needs and believe Him to restore us in body, soul and spirit.

Physical death, for the Christian, is the gateway to resurrection, to the attaining of that full life that is his; the inheritance he has as a child of God. Death becomes the release into the total healing of Jesus, that he has only appropriated partially in this life.

So the Christian has the best of both worlds! He knows that God has done all that is necessary for his wholeness on the Cross, and desires him to appropriate that healing as

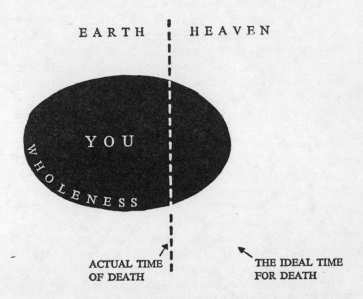

EARTH | HEAVEN

YOU

WHOLENESS

ACTUAL TIME OF DEATH

THE IDEAL TIME FOR DEATH

much as possible now. But death is not failure and defeat; rather the means through which he receives what he has not fully appropriated on earth.

That is not an excuse for complacency. This wholeness is available now, because the Cross is an accomplished fact and "with His stripes *we are healed.*"

God loves you and wants you to glorify Him by revealing His life, His healing, His wholeness, as fully as possible. He wants you to understand that Jesus took your infirmities and bore your diseases. That you can pray with faith about those healing needs in your life, knowing that the Spirit is leading you towards that perfection that God has planned for you.

Your words of faith: "HE TOOK OUR INFIRMITIES AND BORE OUR DISEASES."

24

Setting Free

From Fear

"A GREAT STORM arose on the sea" as Jesus crossed with His disciples (Matt. 8: 24). In their fear and consternation, they awaken Jesus:

> "Save, Lord; we are perishing." And he said to them, "Why are you afraid, O men of little faith?" (Matt. 8: 25–26).

Faith, as Jesus uses that word, is not only what you believe when you pray. It is an attitude to the whole of your life, to all the problems and difficulties that arise. We all know that there will be plenty of them. Jesus does not promise that our lives will be free of problems; but He promises that as we pray with faith, we will see God overcoming them for us.

Faith reduces the size of the mountains. The bigger God is in our hearts, the smaller the mountain will seem.

The fear of the disciples would have been understandable, but for the fact that Jesus was with them. That same Presence who was with them is IN US, who are filled with the Holy Spirit. So Jesus might well say to us: "Why are you afraid, O men of little faith?"

It is so easy to give in to fears, to believe the situation and momentarily forget the Lord; to forget His Presence, and His words of promise. When we remember that He is with us, we ask Him to forgive our faithlessness. He forgives, and we can begin to face the mountain with a new confidence.

The trouble is that some of the difficulties happen suddenly, unexpectedly, like this great storm. Before you know where you are, they are upon you. It is the storms that show each of us clearly how solidly (or not) our lives are built on Jesus. How much (or little) our faith and trust is in Him. Whether we believe our feelings above His Word, or His Word above our feelings of fear, despair, defeat and failure.

God allows the storms to strengthen the foundation of our lives, to build us in faith – not destroy us. He wants us to believe Him to act in the middle of the storms, as the disciples did. Yet even when our prayer is one of desperation: "Save, Lord, we are perishing!", He will hear us. It is a cry that comes from the heart, and God answers the prayers of His children's hearts. "Then he rose and rebuked the winds and the sea; and there was a great calm" (Matt. 8: 26).

Sometimes you will reckon that you have failed the test when your faith is tried. You can take comfort that Jesus often referred to His disciples as "men of little faith" and yet God used them to perform miracles and to be the foundation of His Church after His Ascension.

On other occasions you will rejoice at the outcome of your faith. Remember, God forgives the failures and deserves the credit for the successes. That faith is the result of the Holy Spirit's work within you. And there will be other trials ahead, when once again your faith can be strengthened because you will need to trust Jesus more completely.

From Bondage

There follows the healing of two demoniacs. The demons are commanded to depart with a simple word of authority: "Go".

> So they came out and went into the swine; and behold, the whole herd rushed down the steep bank into the sea, and perished in the waters (Matt. 8: 32).

This shows the destructive power of these evil forces that afflict the lives of some people. It also shows that God's purpose is to set them free. This is another aspect of the total victory that Jesus has over the powers of the enemy; the victory that is made available to us through the Cross.

To see the almighty power of God at work can be an awesome sight: "When they saw him, they begged him to leave their neighbourhood" (v. 34). But how tragic that fear should prevent so many today from ministering the victory of Jesus to those who are bound and need to be set free.

Praise God for the completed and perfect work of the Cross and for every demonstration of His victorious and liberating power.

From Sin and Sickness

Matthew, chapter 9, opens with the account of the paralytic who is brought to Jesus, "lying on his bed".

> And when Jesus SAW THEIR FAITH he said to the paralytic, "Take heart, my son, your sins are forgiven" (v. 2).

Faith is completed only when it results in positive action. That may mean, to pray the prayer of faith, believing God, and waiting faithfully for the fulfilment of the promise. It may mean seeking a time of personal ministry as an occasion when you believe you will receive the answer from Jesus. It may mean some action that God asks of you, a visible evidence of the faith that is within.

It was apparent to Jesus that those who brought the paralytic believed that if they did so, he would be healed. God answers such faith. The men 'knew' that their friend would be healed; that is what Jesus perceived. They were not coming in hope, but with faith.

Jesus tells the man his sins are forgiven. That is the most

crucial and far-reaching act of healing in our lives, restoring us to fellowship with the Father. This underlines the importance of coming to Jesus and giving ourselves whole-heartedly in the healing of our need.

"But that you may know that the Son of man has authority on earth to forgive sins – he then said to the paralytic – "Rise, take up your bed and go home" 9: 6).

Those watching were questioning Jesus' authority. So Jesus speaks again and heals the man of paralysis. The second word of authority is the evidence of the authenticity of the first. It is one aspect of the healing of the Cross, following upon another. Not forgiveness or healing. Forgiveness AND healing.

When the crowds saw the man get up and go home, they were afraid, and they glorified God, who had given such authority to men" (Matt. 9: 8).

And this was an authority that Jesus was to give to His followers.

Jesus Answers Faith

In Matthew 9 verse 18, a ruler *comes* to Jesus, saying:

My daughter has just died; but come and lay your hand on her, and she will live.

That is a statement of faith. A beautiful example of what Jesus teaches about asking: "believe that you have received it, and it will be yours". The child is dead, but the ruler has the faith that if Jesus comes into the situation there is no doubt about the outcome: "she will live"!

Jesus answers the faith that is presented to Him. The centurion believed that Jesus did not even have to come to his house. He only had to speak the word of authority and his servant would be healed. So when He spoke that word, "the servant was healed at that very moment" (Matt. 8: 13).

The ruler's expectation is different: "Come and lay your hand on her, and she will live." That is the faith that is presented to Him, and so that is the faith that Jesus answers. "Jesus rose and followed him, with his disciples" (Matt. 9: 19).

To put it crudely: You get what you expect! That is still true for us today. If we only expect a little, we have no right to be disappointed if we only receive a little. Often we do not aim high enough in our praying, which is an indication that we do not believe 'high enough'.

As Jesus made His way to the ruler's house "a woman who had suffered from a haemorrhage for twelve years came up behind him and touched the fringe of his garment; for she said to herself: If I only touch his garment, I shall be made well" (Matt. 9: 21).

That was the woman's expectancy. That was the faith that she presented to the Lord. There was no 'maybe' about it. "I SHALL BE MADE WELL."

The centurion believed that his faith would be answered by a word of authority from Jesus.

The ruler believed that his faith would be answered by the touch of Jesus' hand.

This woman believed her faith would be answered by touching the clothing of Jesus.

Jesus answers all three methods. Why? Because He is not interested in the method, but answering the faith of each one.

That is God's way with you. He will answer what you believe – always.

Jesus turns to the woman and says to her: "Take heart, daughter, your faith has made you well. Instantly the woman was made well" (Matt. 9: 22).

"Your faith has made you well." That is the power of faith. We are not to have faith in our faith! Our trust is to be

in Jesus. The woman had faith, not in herself, not in her own
faith, but *in Jesus* to heal her. He is saying to her: "Your
faith in me to heal you has made you well."

When Jesus arrives at the ruler's house, He dismisses the
mourners and then: "He took her by the hand, and the girl
arose" (v. 25). Jesus has answered the faith of the ruler. He
has come. He has touched her with His hand. She lives.

It is impossible to have the kind of faith demonstrated by
those who came to Jesus, unless you really believe that God
wants to heal you, or the one for whom you pray. If there is
any doubt about God's will to heal, you cannot pray the
prayer of faith. That is why it is so important to understand
healing in relation to all that Jesus has already accomplished
on the Cross.

Do not be afraid to bring your need to Jesus. Your prayer
may be a cry from the heart, a cry of desperation. He will
hear you and will answer.

Your coming may be more calculated like that of the centurion, the ruler, or the woman. Jesus will reward your faith
and give you what you believe.

He *wants* you to come. He *wants* you to ask. He *wants* to
answer. He *wants* to give.

**Your words of faith: "TAKE HEART, MY SON; YOUR
SINS ARE FORGIVEN." "TAKE HEART, MY DAUGH-
TER, YOUR FAITH HAS MADE YOU WELL."**

25

Do You Believe?

AND AS JESUS passed on from there, two blind men followed him, crying aloud, "Have mercy on us, Son of David" (Matt.9: 27).

The way to approach Jesus is to say: "Have mercy on us". We need to hear His words of forgiveness, before any other word of healing.

We can never come to Jesus deserving to be healed, as if it is our right. True, we come as the new covenant children, knowing the love and faithfulness of our Father. True, we come knowing that every promise of Jesus will be fulfilled, when we believe Him. That still does not mean that we *deserve* to be healed or forgiven. We don't deserve to receive anything from God.

It is only out of His abounding graciousness that He desires to give to His children.

I regularly receive letters from people asking me to pray for their Christian friends or relatives. Many of these letters list the loving qualities of the sick person and hint at the seeming injustice that they should be ill at all, because they are such good people. It is suggested that the Lord surely wants to heal such loving and saintly children.

It is certainly true that God wants to heal His children. But His healing does not come as a reward for our goodness, or love, or saintliness. It comes out of His loving and generous heart and is given to those who *deserve nothing*. Children of God we are, but we still sin. We still disobey. We still grieve our heavenly Father. We still need His forgiveness and His mercy. That is why whenever we are seeking healing for ourselves or others, we do so through the Cross.

The two blind men came to Him and Jesus puts a test question to them: "Do you believe that I am able to do this?" (Matt. 9: 28).

Do you BELIEVE? Jesus is not asking a theoretical or academic question. He is not saying, "Do you believe that it is within my powers to heal you one day?" He does not mean, "Do you believe I can do such things?"

He is saying: "Do you believe me TO DO IT?"

The blind men give a simple answer of faith, "Yes, Lord."

Is it really that simple? Yes, it is – when there is the kind of faith that Jesus talks about.

Testing Questions

Several years ago, when I first began to minister the healing of Jesus to those who came, I learned to ask simple test questions, to draw out people's faith. I might say casually: "It's going to happen, isn't it?" Or, "Jesus is going to heal you, isn't He?"

Usually the answer would be the simple statement of faith; "Yes, He is," or "I believe He is." There would be a calmness and a quiet assurance in the answer. A 'knowing'. The time of preparation (coming to the Cross and 'receiving' the promises) was important to bring people to that point of simple expectancy.

However, on some occasions, instead of a simple statement of faith, there would be a telling pause, followed by such a phrase as: "Well, I hope so!"

Hope is not faith. In such situations faith needs to be ministered to that person, before healing. There is no point in rushing into prayer and "hoping for the best". It is better to encourage the person to face honestly their doubts and bring them to the Cross; to point them to the promises of the Lord and His faithfulness. Some people are healed gradually, and receive ministry on a number of occasions, because God is having to build faith and expectancy all the time.

On a few occasions, in answer to the test question, people have gone into a tirade: "Oh, I believe He is. He really is. Oh, He's given me so much assurance. I have such faith that He is going to do it ..." The longer they go on, the more obvious it becomes that they do not really believe that God is going to heal them. They are trying to encourage faith within themselves. If they believed in the way they professed, the healing would have happened already.

These are usually the most difficult situations to deal with, because the person thinks he believes, when it is apparent that he doesn't. Again, there is no point in rushing into the laying on of hands. Real faith has to be ministered first.

According to Your Faith

The two blind men have that simple, quiet 'knowing' that it will be done. And Jesus "touched their eyes, saying, 'According to your FAITH be it done to you' " (Matt. 9: 29).

According to your FAITH ... He keeps saying the same thing in different ways!

To the Roman centurion Jesus says: "Go; be it done for you, AS YOU HAVE BELIEVED" (Matt. 8: 13).

To the woman with the haemorrhage, Jesus says: "Take heart, daughter; your faith has made you well" (Matt. 9: 22).

To the two blind men, Jesus says: "According to your faith be it done to you" (Matt. 9: 29).

To the Canaanite woman, Jesus says: "O woman great is your faith! Be it done for you as you desire" (Matt. 15: 28).

To blind Bartimaeus, Jesus says: "Go your way, your faith has made you well" (Mark 10: 52).

To the leper who returned to give thanks Jesus says: "Rise and go your way; your faith has made you well" (Luke 17: 19).

Authority

After the incident with the two blind men, a dumb de-moniac was *brought* to him. And when the demon had been cast out, the dumb man spoke; and the crowd marvelled, saying, "Never was anything like this seen in Israel" (Matt. 9: 32–33).

When the problem was one of demon possession, Jesus does not elicit faith from the person; He uses His own faith and authority to deal with the matter.

"But the Pharisees said, He casts out demons by the prince of demons" (v. 34). Of course, if you don't want to believe, you won't. Any excuse will do as a justification for unbelief.

Every Disease

> And Jesus went about all the cities and villages, teach-ing in their synagogues and preaching the gospel of the kingdom, and healing every disease and every infirmity (Matt. 9: 35).

"EVERY disease and EVERY infirmity", because he took *all* our infirmities and bore *all* our diseases. Yet Jesus does not separate the healing from His preaching of the kingdom of God. "Seek first his kingdom and his righteous-ness, and all these things shall be yours as well" (Matt. 6: 33).

If our concern is to seek His Father's kingdom first in our lives and to be in a right relationship with Him, Jesus prom-ises our needs *will* be met. We will not need to be anxious about anything.

Jesus passed on to the disciples not only His commission to preach the Gospel, but also the same authority and power.

And he called to him twelve disciples and gave them authority over unclean spirits, to cast them out, and to heal every disease and every infirmity (Matt. 10: 1).

"EVERY disease and EVERY infirmity!" The authority of this commission to His followers was not for the time of the ministry of Jesus alone, but extended through the apostolic church and the centuries of Christendom until the present day. It extends into the future until Jesus returns, according to His promise, when all the healing of God in the lives of His children will be completed.

Now many signs and wonders were done among the people by the hands of the apostles ... they even carried the sick out into the streets, and laid them on beds and pallets, that as Peter came by at least his shadow might fall on some of them. The people also gathered from the towns around Jerusalem, bringing the sick and those afflicted with unclean spirits and they were healed (Acts 5: 12, 15–16).

Those were days of expectant faith. And whenever among God's people today that same expectant faith re-emerges, the healing power of God is seen at work again. What we are witnessing of the renewing power of God at work within His Church at present is only a beginning compared with what needs to be seen, with what God, our Father, wants for us.

Your Healing

Jesus asks you the same question as He asked the two blind men: "Do you believe I am able to do this?" Answer Him honestly. Where you know there is doubt, be open with God about it. Ask the Holy Spirit to witness the prayer and healing promises of the Lord to your heart. When you *know*

He wants to heal you, pray the prayer of faith and hold on to your Father's promises until your answer has arrived.

Your words of faith: "DO YOU BELIEVE I AM ABLE TO DO THIS?"

26

Hearing With Faith

ST. PAUL ASKS: "Did you receive the Spirit by works of the law, or by hearing with faith?" (Gal. 3: 2). By "hearing with faith", of course!

"Does he who supplies the Spirit to you and works miracles among you do so by works of the law, or by hearing with faith?" (Gal. 3: 5). By "hearing with faith", of course.

It makes no sense to say that the Holy Spirit was only poured out in power upon the Church in the time of the apostles, and that miracles belong only to that period of the Church's history. Paul makes it clear that both were the result of "hearing with faith". An absence of either the Spirit's power or the mighty works of God anywhere in the Church, is evidence, not that God is withholding His Spirit and His works, but that there is no longer "hearing with faith".

With the coming of Jesus Christ and the establishing of the new covenant came the age of the Spirit, the era of faith. *Through faith*, the Galatians received the inheritance of Abraham and could enter into all the old covenant promises. *Through faith* in Jesus Christ they had received the precious gift of the Holy Spirit. *Through faith* they saw God working miracles among them.

And yet Paul cries: "O foolish Galatians! Who has bewitched you?" For having tasted the freedom of the Holy Spirit and His mighty power at work amongst them, they were already returning to their conventional religious attitudes. Paul knew that there could be no more serious deviation from the truth of the Gospel. As soon as the working of Jesus Christ by the power of His Spirit becomes limited by Christian legalism, faith immediately dwindles, and the receiving of all that God wants to give His children, diminishes.

Christian 'Law'

Many church-going people have been brought up with a very legalistic view of Christianity. Traditions are exalted above the Word of God and create the attitude of 'no change' within the life of the Church. The future is to be bound by the law of "what we have done in the past". The mind is exalted above waiting upon the Spirit for His direction concerning the life and affairs of the congregation. It becomes more important to have the right doctrine, than the right life. The Bible is treated as God's Law book.

Many congregations settle into a routine way of life, where the system is perpetuated week by week, month by month, year by year – just as for centuries Israel observed her feasts and did the works of the law.

Where is the vibrant faith of the new covenant? Where are the promises of God being fulfilled among His people? Where does the Holy Spirit have His rightful place of leadership within the Church?

The Spirit is the mighty wind of God that needs to blow freely through the life of His Church and the individual lives of His children. The Spirit is the One who will inspire faith. And yet so often the mind is allowed to stifle the working of the Spirit. That is what happens when people hold on to their conventional, legalistic attitudes, and think more highly of their 'party' attitudes than the Word of God.

Either the Spirit will be allowed to inform the mind; or the mind will stifle the Spirit.

A New Approach

Jesus taught His disciples to approach problems, not with an intellectual appraisal of the situation, but with a spiritual attitude. In other words, not by saying "What can we do here?" but rather, "What can God do?" The feeding of the multitude is a good example.

A great crowd of people had been following Jesus "because they saw the signs which he did on those who were diseased" (John 6: 2). He puts a test question to Philip:

> "How are we to buy bread, so that these people may eat?" This he said to test him, for he himself knew what he would do (John 6: 5–6).

Jesus begins at Philip's level. He knows that the disciple will approach the situation with his mind, rather than with the eyes of faith. It is his faith that is being tested! "Philip answered him, Two hundred denarii would not buy enough bread for each of them to get a little" (v. 7).

That is the answer of the mind; a good, sound, logical appraisal of the situation. Andrew's attitude is similar: "Andrew, Simon Peter's brother, said to him, 'There is a lad here who has five barley loaves and two fish, but what are they among so many?' " (vv. 8–9).

True. But neither statement takes into account that Jesus is at hand!

> Jesus then took the loaves, and when he had given thanks, he distributed them to those who were seated; so also the fish as MUCH AS THEY WANTED (v. 11).

He is the One who can take a paltry, insignificant offering and multiply it, so that it meets not only the *needs* of people but satisfies all they *want*. He told the disciples to gather up all the fragments left over and they filled twelve baskets; one for each of them. No doubt that rubbed the lesson home! From being defeated by the enormity of the task when they approached it with their minds, they now feast on the abundance of what Jesus has provided by the Spirit.

Every Problem is a Spiritual Problem

Jesus approached every situation from a spiritual angle. We often limit the working of God because we consider the problem with our minds, instead of "hearing with faith" what our Father is able to accomplish, through the promises of His Word.

If your Christian life depends upon your rational thinking, then you will limit God to the level of your mind. You make Him smaller than yourself. In truth, He is infinitely greater, and His power is beyond your understanding, beyond anything that your mind can conceive.

You will need to learn to approach each situation, not with the limitation of your mind, but seeing the potential of the Spirit. Often the mind will encourage a negative, defeatist attitude. "This situation is hopeless. So many people to feed. A vast sum of money would be needed – if we had it! All we have is a small boy's picnic. What good is that for all these people?"

The Spirit will encourage faith, believing God to turn the problem into an opportunity to witness His hand at work; to see His glory revealed among His people. The Spirit will declare God's word to you.

No amount of intellectualising will produce a miracle or an answer to prayer.

What is to be the relationship between the mind and Spirit then? *The mind is to be submitted to the Spirit, for the Spirit will enlarge your mind and expand your thinking to include the 'impossible' things of God.*

The Conflict

Paul speaks of the conflict between the Spirit and the 'flesh'. We have been baptised into the death of Jesus; he has taken us to the Cross and we have been crucified with Him, so that we might no longer live as the people we once were, believing our lives to be our own, bound by fear, and sin, full of doubt, unbelief and ignorance of God's love for us and the promises that He wants to fulfil in our lives.

> We know that our old self was crucified with him so that the sinful body might be destroyed, and we might no longer be enslaved to sin (Rom. 6: 6).

That 'old self', the 'flesh', the person you were before you met personally with Jesus Christ, is dead and buried. You are now a new creature, a child of God. Instead of being 'enslaved to sin', you now have Jesus living in you. He is the centre of your new being, of your new life.

The apostle gives three clear directions, to enable people to live freely in the power of the Spirit, to believe and to see the promises of God fulfilled in their lives.

First Direction: "Consider yourselves dead"

> You also must consider yourselves dead to sin and alive to God in Christ Jesus (Rom. 6: 11).

You MUST consider yourselves DEAD to that old life where sin dominated, and ALIVE TO GOD IN CHRIST JESUS. You live in Jesus, because that is where the Father has placed you. In His beloved Son. In the Vine. You are a child of God no longer alienated from Him by your sin, but called, accepted, washed clean by the blood of the Cross. You are a child of the new covenant and all God's promises are your inheritance.

Let not sin therefore reign in your mortal bodies, to
make you obey their passions. Do not yield your
members to sin as instruments of wickedness, but
YIELD YOURSELVES TO GOD as men who have
been brought from death to life, and your members to
God as instruments of righteousness (Rom. 6: 12–13).

Second Direction: "Yield yourselves to God"

It is not enough to have acknowledged at some point in
the past that your life belongs to God. You need to live as
someone whose life is 'yielded' to God. This means:
You want His will above your own.
You want to give him glory in every aspect of your life.
You are living to give yourself to Him in praise and wor-
ship, and in loving service of others.
You are living to be like him, a 'giving' person.

As you continue to yield yourself to God, to give yourself
to Him so you will be able to receive what He desires to give
to you. Paul warns: "you are slaves of the one whom you
obey, either of sin, which leads to death, or of obedience,
which leads to righteousness" (Rom 6: 16).

So don't obey your own selfish desires, your sinful
passions. Don't obey your doubts, your fears and feelings of
inadequacy. Obey the Spirit, for He speaks faith to you.

But thanks be to God, that you who were once slaves of
sin have become obedient from the heart to the standard of teaching to which you were committed (v. 17).

Don't reduce God in size and say: "He can do only what I
experience Him doing." He wants your experience raised to
the "standard of teaching to which you were committed", to
the teaching of His Word by the Holy Spirit, that you might
"hear with faith".

"Obedient from the heart" because under the terms of the

new convenant, you now have a 'new heart' with the law of
God written upon it. You have a new spirit, with God's
Spirit living within you, to cause you to walk in obedience to
him.

Third Direction: "Set Your Mind on the Things of the Spirit"

> Those who live according to the flesh set their minds on
> the things of the flesh, but those who live according to
> the Spirit set their minds on the things of the Spirit. To
> set the mind on the flesh is death, but to set the mind on
> the Spirit is life and peace. For the mind that is set on
> the flesh is hostile to God; it does not submit to God's
> law, indeed it cannot; and those who are in the flesh
> cannot please God (Rom 8: 5–8).

Although you have the Spirit of Jesus living in you, there
will be many temptations to return to a life "in the flesh",
putting yourself first, believing your fears, doubts and feelings of failure, having a negative attitude to your problems.
But Paul reminds you:

> You are not in the flesh, you are in the Spirit, if in fact
> the Spirit of God dwells in you (Rom. 8: 9).

As you set your mind on the things of the Spirit, your
attitude to life will become more positive, because you will
learn to look at every situation with the eyes of Jesus, knowing that your Father is prepared to give to you. Your mind
will be enlarged by the Spirit to include the impossible!

> For all who are led by the Spirit of God are sons of
> God. For you did not receive the spirit of slavery to fall
> back into fear, but you have received the spirit of son-
> ship. When we cry, "Abba! Father!" it is the Spirit
> himself bearing witness with our spirit that we are

children of God, and if children, then heirs, heirs of God and fellow heirs with Christ, provided we suffer with him in order that we may also be glorified with him (8: 14–17).

To follow the leading of the Spirit is to live as a son of God, His new covenant child. In every situation you can cry 'Father' and know that He hears you; He cares, He loves and He will answer you.

To set your mind on the 'flesh' is to take your eyes off 'Father', the source of life and love, the only one who can meet your needs.

God does not want you to be a 'mindless' Christian, with a non-intellectual approach to your faith in Him. Rather, He wants to fill your mind with His thoughts and rejoice that your intellect has been offered to Him to become a consecrated intellect, understanding more fully the ways of your heavenly Father.

Your words of faith: "THROUGH GOD YOU ARE NO LONGER A SLAVE BUT A SON, AND IF A SON THEN AN HEIR" (Gal. 4: 4–6).

27

In Giving You Receive

"THE MEASURE YOU give will be the measure you get," says Jesus (Matt. 7: 2). That is true of your dealings with God, it is true also of your relationships with other people. "Whatever you wish that men would do to you, do so to them" Matt. 7: 12).

Jesus demonstrated a life of giving; He came to show His Father's desire to give out of His great love for His creation:

> For God so LOVED the world that he GAVE his only Son, that whoever believes in him should not perish but have eternal life (John 3: 16).

Jesus has made you acceptable to the Father, and has filled you with the Holy Spirit. Before you could receive this rich inheritance, you had to come to the Cross and *give* yourself to the Lord. Many people do not have the relationship with God that they desire, because they have not given themselves to God, for that fellowship to be established.

When we give, it is God's way to give back.

> Give and it will be given to you; good measure, pressed down, shaken together, running over, will be put into your lap. For the measure you give will be the measure you get back (Luke 6: 38).

We give God our lives; He gives back His life.

We give God our sin and failure; He gives back forgiveness and peace.

We give God our bodies; He gives back His Holy Spirit and makes those bodies His temples.

That is God's way. Give and He will give.

Jesus teaches that it is important to give to others, if you expect to receive from God. For example, you are to forgive others in order to receive the forgiveness that God wants to give you. "Forgive, and you will be forgiven" (Luke 6: 37). Forgive others FIRST, and then God will forgive you.

We do not mind giving away sin if we obtain forgiveness from God. We do not object to giving Him our fears and anxieties, if He is going to take them away from us. We do not mind being rid of our dirt, if we are going to be made clean as a result. It is one thing to give away what we do not want. It is another to give what is precious or valuable to us. Our minds immediately caution us against giving away what is of value, because to give implies that we are going to lose something.

We want to lose sin and failure; we want to lose fear and anxiety; we want to lose pain and sickness.

We don't want to lose money or property; we don't want to lose time or control of our lives; we don't want to lose our independence.

Jesus teaches us that it is only in losing that we shall gain. That offends our thinking. By choice it would not be our way. *It is God's Way.*

> Whoever would save his life will lose it, and whoever loses his life for my sake will find it. For what will it profit a man, if he gains the whole world and forfeits his life? Or what shall a man give in return for his life?' (Matt. 16: 25–26).

This is God's way – no matter what we think about it. He is saying to us that it is only in giving away that we are going to receive.

Faith is like a two-sided coin. 'Believe' is on one side; 'give' on the other. Put the two together and you have the way open for successful prayer. For time and time again, your faith will be tested by God asking you to give before you receive. Are you prepared to trust Him to fulfil His Word so that you do not end up the loser, but the one who has gained because you have approached the problem, not with your mind controlling events, but according to God's way?

Your mind will tell you that you will lose, that you do not need to give. God tells you that you will receive and that you do need to give. Who are you going to believe?

Sowing and Reaping

The imagery of the sower and the seed is used extensively in the New Testament to teach the importance of giving before expecting to receive. St. Paul says:

> The point is this; he who sows sparingly will also reap sparingly, and he who sows bountifully will also reap bountifully (2 Cor. 9: 6).

A farmer knows that he has to sow seeds before there will be a harvest. He has to give to the soil before he can expect to receive back from it. If he only sows sparsely, he will receive a poor crop. If he sows plenty of seed there will be a much better harvest.

The quality of the seed is also important. If he sows poor quality seed, he will receive a poor quality harvest. If he sows the best, he will receive a harvest rich in quality.

So a farmer will sow plenty of seed of the best quality, and then *expect* his harvest to be good.

God wants each of us to be 'good farmers'. He wants to teach us to give plentifully – of our best. Because this is God's way of working. He kept to it Himself when He sent His Son. He gave of His very best. He gave Himself. He wanted a rich harvest. He gave the best Seed. And Jesus Himself said:

Truly, truly, I say to you, unless a grain of wheat falls into the earth and dies, it remains alone; but if it dies, it bears much fruit (John 12: 24).

The Father not only gave the best Seed; that Seed had to die in order to be fruitful to restore men to God's kingdom.

Only by 'dying' to self will we be able to live for God and be fruitful in the way that He desires. Only by losing our lives, do we gain His life and the rich inheritance that He has for us as His children. The best seed is costly. To sow plentifully is costly. And so our minds say: "Don't do it. You will lose!"

The Spirit urges us: "Do it. You will gain!" That is why so many people have a time of great tension and turmoil before their conversion, or before seeking the release of the Holy Spirit in their lives.

Each one must do as he has made up his mind, not reluctantly or under compulsion, for God loves a cheerful giver (2 Cor. 9: 7).

An Abundant Harvest

You have to make up your mind whether you are going to trust God or your own human thinking. And God does not want you to give to Him begrudgingly, but out of a heart that overflows with love for Him and for others. God does not give begrudgingly to you; He gives out of His love and concern for you. He gives because He wants to provide for you.

And God is able to provide you with every blessing in abundance, so that you may always have enough of everything and may provide in abundance for every good work (2 Cor. 9: 8).

That is God's way. He wants to provide for YOU in

ABUNDANCE. Not meagrely, not miserly. In ABUN-
DANCE.

Your mind will often tell you that God does not want
to give you, that you are unworthy. If He does give, it will
only be the bare minimum to meet your greatest needs,
to "see you through". God says that He wants to provide
for YOU in ABUNDANCE. Not a little bit of blessing
here and there, occasionally. His Word says: "EVERY
BLESSING – so that YOU may ALWAYS have enough of
everything."

ALWAYS!
ENOUGH OF EVERYTHING!

Somehow we Christians have exalted poverty and depri-
vation. And all the time our God is the God of love, the
ABUNDANT GIVER of EVERY BLESSING, so that we
ALWAYS have enough of EVERYTHING.

Why don't we manifest this abundance? Because it only
happens when we learn to *give* first and *believe* God for the
abundance that He promises.

Not that God wants to provide for self-indulgence. He
will "provide in abundance *for every good work*". He gives
freely and in abundance to us, in order that we may give
freely and in abundance to others.

God's Way

How difficult it is to understand the ways of God with the
mind! The committees of so many churches demonstrate
their lack of faith by approaching their finances like any
worldly organisation. They do not believe God's way; that
you give first, even out of your poverty, and then expect
God to give of His abundance. They think so poorly of such
an idea that many have never done it. They have not walked
by faith. It is unreasonable. Others have, and have witnessed
the faithfulness of God.

He who supplies seed to the sower and bread for food will supply and multiply your resources and increase the harvest of your righteousness (2 Cor. 9: 10).

Do you believe this? And believing means that you will not only hear it, and agree with it, but that *you will act upon it.*

Paul says that God "will supply and multiply your resources". But first the seed has to be sown, to be given to the ground. Every seed produces a whole ear of corn, containing many seeds. That is God's way of taking what is given and multiplying it back. But not for our own self-indulgence!

You will be enriched in every way for great generosity, which through us will produce great thanksgiving to God (v. 11).

The more that God supplies to His children, the more they have to give to others. And God is prepared to give EVERY BLESSING IN ABUNDANCE.

He will give His love, that we might overflow with love and service to others. He will give His power that we might be instruments through which His power can be ministered to others. He will even give to us financially so that we will have plenty to give.

The richer the harvest, the more seed there is to put back into the ground: to give to God. And He will multiply that back in even greater abundance, that not only we, but all who receive through us, will rejoice and be thankful to Him.

For the rendering of this service not only supplies the wants of the saints but also overflows in many thanksgivings to God (v. 12).

God will provide many opportunities for you to give, whether directly to Him, or to others. In giving to others, you will be giving to Him.

There will be opportunities to love and serve; to give yourself to God in praise; to pray believing prayers for the needs of others; to give to the work of the Gospel; to give to others.

How we respond to such opportunities will be a real test of our faith, especially when we have little time, or ability, or money to offer for the situation placed before us. Paul is writing to the Corinthians about one such situation where they needed to give financially. The principle is the same in every area of our Christian lives; it is in giving that we receive.

> Under the test of this service, you will glorify God of your obedience in acknowledging the gospel of Christ, and by the *generosity* of your contribution for them and for all others (v. 13).

When the angel of the Lord spoke to Cornelius, he said: "Your prayers and your alms have ascended as a memorial before God" (Acts 10: 4). And what harvest did the Lord give back to Cornelius? He sent Peter to his house and the Holy Spirit fell upon all who heard him speak, including Cornelius.

This is not to imply that we can buy blessing from God! As he had been faithful in praying and giving to God, so God was faithful in answering his prayers and giving to him.

The spiritual poverty of many people is shown by a marked unwillingness to give:

Of themselves; "I don't want to get involved."

Of their time; "I'm so busy"

Of their abilities; "I couldn't."

Of their money; "It's all I can afford."

Of their prayer; "I don't seem to get any answers."

Of their worship; "It better be finished within the hour."

People want to receive. Their minds tell them that they ought to receive, that they have the right to receive. And so often they are left wondering why they don't receive.

Like the farmer, when you plant seed you have to wait for the harvest. The crop is not available immediately. And many of the problems are in the time of waiting. It is so easy to give up.

The farmer is expectant. He is always looking for the signs of the coming harvest. As you pray, believing the promises of God, have the same expectancy. Give to the One who will supply all your needs, in the way that you believe He is asking of you. And expect the harvest; keep looking for the signs that the seeds of giving you have planted are being multiplied back to you by your loving Father who teaches you ...

Your words of faith: "GIVE AND IT SHALL BE GIVEN TO YOU; GOOD MEASURE, PRESSED DOWN, SHAKEN TOGETHER, RUNNING OVER, WILL BE PUT INTO YOUR LAP. FOR THE MEASURE YOU GIVE WILL BE THE MEASURE YOU GET BACK."

28

Believing Ground

THE FARMER IS concerned with the quality of the ground
as well as the seed he puts into it.

God gives His Word to us as a seed. He wants that Word
to produce a rich harvest of His giving to us. The 'soil'
quality of our lives will determine how fruitful that Word is.

> A sower went out to sow his seed; and as he sowed,
> some fell along the path, and was trodden underfoot,
> and the birds of the air devoured it (Luke 8: 5).

In the interpretation of the parable, Jesus said:

> The ones along the path are those who have heard; then
> the devil comes and takes away the word from their
> hearts, that they may not believe and be saved (Luke
> 8: 12).

Satan is the thief who wants to steal, destroy and kill. He
delights in encouraging us to disbelieve the Word. "The
ones along the path" are those who do not even begin to believe that God will give to them.

> And some fell on the rocks; and as it grew up, it with-
> ered away, because it had no moisture (Luke 8: 6).
> And the ones on the rock are those who, when they
> hear the word, receive it with joy; but these have no
> root, they believe for a while and in time of temptation
> fall away (Luke 8: 13).

There is no depth to their faith. They believe at first, but when the going gets tough they easily give up. They believe their doubts and fears.

Whenever you are believing God for an answer to prayer, the tempter will encourage you to doubt. You will have to use the "shield of faith, with which you can quench all the flaming darts of the evil one" (Eph. 6: 16).

> And some fell among thorns; and the thorns grew with it and choked it (Luke 8: 7).
> And as for what fell among the thorns, they are those who hear, but as they go on their way they are choked by the cares and riches and pleasures of life, and their fruit does not mature (Luke 8: 14).

You cannot isolate your prayers from the rest of your life. Their fruitfulness will depend largely upon the kind of life you are living; whether you live to give to God, or whether you are still living for yourself, "choked by cares and riches and pleasures of life." Whether you only want to receive, or become a generous giver.

It is not only worldliness that 'chokes' the seed; Jesus says it is also choked by 'cares'. By problems, worries, anxiety, fear. All these things are the opposite of faith.

> And some fell into good soil and grew, and yielded a hundredfold (Luke 8: 8).
> And as for that in the good soil, they are those who, hearing the word, hold it fast in an honest and good heart, and bring forth fruit with patience (Luke 8: 15).

The fruitful hearers are the believers. They not only hear the word; they *hold it fast*, no matter what the situation, no matter how many doubts are pushed in their direction. They hold on to the promise of God. They believe Him.

Their believing comes from the heart. And they *bring forth fruit with patience*. They wait for the fulfilment of the promises of God, knowing that He will be faithful.

Differences

There is an interesting difference in the version of the parable given in St. Luke's Gospel, from that in Matthew and Mark. Matthew reads:

> As for what was sown on good soil, this is he who hears the word and understands it; he indeed bears fruit, and yields, in one case a hundredfold, in another sixty, and in another thirty (Matt. 13: 23).

The productivity varies for he who "hears the word *and understands it*". And apparently diminishes. Mark reads:

> But those that were sown upon the good soil are the ones who hear the word and accept it and bear fruit, thirtyfold and sixtyfold and a hundredfold (Mark 4: 20).

The productivity varies for "those who hear the word *and accept it*". And apparently increases. As their acceptance grows, so does the level of fruitfulness in their lives.

In Luke's account those in the good soil are those who "hearing the word, hold it fast in an honest and good heart, and bring forth fruit with patience".

And the only level of productivity mentioned in Luke is "a hundredfold". Those who "hold fast" the word are consistent in their yield, and it is the highest yield. No wonder Jesus said:

> Take heed how you hear; for to him who has will more be given, and from him who has not, even what he thinks that he has will be taken away (Luke 8: 18).

Take heed HOW you hear. Hold the promises fast with an

honest and good heart, before God and man. And see the Lord's harvest in your life.

> You did not choose me, but I chose you and appointed you that you should go and bear fruit and that your fruit should abide; so that WHATEVER you ask the Father in my name, he may give it to you (John 15: 16).

Your words of faith: "HEARING THE WORD, HOLD IT FAST IN AN HONEST AND GOOD HEART, AND BRING FORTH FRUIT WITH PATIENCE."

29

The Heart of the Matter

THE 'GOOD SOIL' in which God plants His seed, consists of those who "hearing the word, hold it fast in an honest and good *heart*, and bring forth fruit with patience". There is much in the teaching of Jesus about 'the heart', which has an important bearing on the fruitfulness of our prayers. He said:

> No good tree bears bad fruit, nor again does a bad tree bear good fruit; for each tree is known by its own fruit (Luke 6: 43–44).

If you want to see good fruit, you need to be concerned with the health of the tree. It is no use looking for the best quality fruit on a tree that is bad. The tree, Jesus says, is the heart.

> The good man *out of the good treasure of his heart* produces good, and the evil man out of his evil treasure produces evil; for out of the abundance of the heart his mouth speaks (v. 45).

Our Father wants us to have loving, obedient hearts. Jesus continued: 'Why do you call me Lord, Lord, and not do what I tell you?" (v. 46).

Love Involves Obedience

> If I have all faith, so as to remove mountains, but have not love, I am nothing. If I give away all that I have . . . but have not love, I gain nothing (1 Cor. 13: 2–3).

Without love, our believing and giving will come to nothing. Paul is not putting alternatives before us: either you love, or you believe and give. We are to love and believe and give. Believing and giving that is without love will 'gain nothing', it will not result in receiving.

"If you love me", Jesus said, "you will keep my commandments" (John 14: 15); you will be obedient to me.

> If you keep my commandments, you will abide in my love, just as I have kept my Father's commandments and abide in His love (John 15: 10).

Jesus prayed within a relationship of loving obedience to His Father, knowing that His Father would hear and answer Him. That love was manifested in the way in which He gave Himself to others. So John says:

> Beloved, let us love one another; for love is of God, and he who loves is born of God and knows God. He who does not love does not know God, for God is love. (I John 4: 7–8).
> If we love one another, God abides in us and his love is perfected in us (4: 12).

God has put His resources of love within us, by the power of His Holy Spirit. It is no use having His love, unless we allow it to be released in our lives; unless we give it to others.

Living Water

> Jesus stood up and proclaimed, "If any one thirst, let him come to me and drink. He who believes in me, as the scripture has said, 'Out of his heart shall flow rivers of living water.' " Now this he said about the Spirit, which those who believe in him were to receive (John 7: 37–39).

God wants the river of His love to flow out from our hearts, from the depths within us, expressed in our giving to one another.

God wants the river of praise and worship to flow from deep within us. That may be a quietly flowing river; it may be a noisy, rushing river. But God wants it to be a *full* river, expressing our love for Him.

God wants the river of joy to flow from within us, even in the most trying circumstances, because we know the love, the care and the faithfulness of our Father.

God wants the river of peace to flow from deep within us, so that we do not become anxious and fearful, but trust Him and rest in Him.

God wants the river of power to flow from within us, into every situation; so that we are not overcome and defeated but learn to use His resources.

God wants the river of faith to flow from our hearts, believing Him to act generously in His love.

God wants the river of healing to flow from the depths of our being, making us whole in body, mind and spirit.

God wants all these rivers of life to flow from within us, out of us and all around us, so that others become influenced by:

> the love of God within us;
> the praise of God on our lips;
> the joy of God in our hearts;
> the peace of God in our souls;
> the power of God in our praying;
> the faith of God in our attitudes;
> the healing of God as we forgive and reach out to others with His love.

These "rivers of living water" are the Spirit at work within us. They flow from the heart. God is not concerned about our doctrines of the Holy Spirit; He wants to see the reality of those "rivers of living water" in our loving, our praise and worship, our joyful hearts, our peace, our powerful praying, our faithful attitudes, our whole and healthy lives and our generous giving. God does not want us to 'possess' those rivers. He wants them continually flowing out from within us. He wants to see the love flowing by our obedience to Him and our service to others. He wants to see the faith causing us to "hold fast" to the words and promises of God "in an honest and good heart".

Faith with love!

Love with faith!

Selfishness can stop the flowing out of love to others. Resentment, bitterness, pride, jealousy all have the same effect. And when one river becomes blocked, the flow of the others can easily be disrupted. That is why Jesus said:

> And whenever you stand praying, forgive, if you have anything against anyone; so that your Father also who is in heaven may forgive you your trespasses (Mark 11: 25).

Our ability to pray with faith and see God answering is hampered by wrong relationships with others.

> If you are offering your gift at the altar, and there remember that your brother has something against you, leave your gift there before the altar and go; first be reconciled to your brother, and then come and offer your gift (Matt. 5: 23–24).

It is not easy to feel full of faith:

> if you know that you are being unloving to someone.
> if there is little praise in your heart for God;
> if there is little joy within you;
> if there is anxiety instead of peace;
> if there is doubt instead of trust in God's power.

You do not pray in a vacuum. That prayer comes out of

the person you are and the relationships you have with God and with others. That does not mean that you should stop praying because you feel empty or inadequate. When you know faith is lacking, ask God to show you what is blocking the flow of the "rivers of living water" from out of your heart.

He may point to any one of many reasons; a bad relationship, unloving attitudes, selfishness, lack of praise, anxiety, lack of giving or one of many others. It is things like these that the Lord often sorts out during the time of 'waiting' for a prayer promise to be fulfilled.

Like me, you would probably like 'rockets' every time you prayed. Often the 'tortoises' are far more valuable, not only because God builds faith in us as we continue to trust Him, but also because He uses the opportunity to sort out many things in our lives.

People are complex, and one problem can easily affect so many others in our lives. It is generally accepted that a high proportion of physical disorders are caused by mental stress of one kind or another. It is certainly true that spiritual sickness can prevent our receiving physical and emotional healing. That is why every time we come to the Lord wanting to receive, we need to be prepared to give first. Give the sin, the failure, the doubt, the emptiness, the tension, the anxiety, the troubled relationships, as well as the positive offering of ourselves.

God does not demand that we reach a stage of spiritual perfection before He gives to us; He does require us to be open and honest with Him, letting Him forgive and put right what is wrong. He accepts us as we are and changes us into what He wants us to be.

Unbelief is the cause of many prayers seeming to be powerless and unfruitful. Lack of love for God or others has a similar effect. God always wants to get to the heart of the matter. And that often means our own hearts.

What comes out of a man is what defiles a man. For

from within, *out of the heart of man*, come evil thoughts, fornication, theft, murder, adultery, coveting, wickedness, deceit, licentiousness, envy, slander, pride, foolishness. All these evil things come from within, and they defile a man (Mark 7: 20–23).

That list contains things that are obviously evil and others that are socially more acceptable, but still 'defile' us and therefore the power of our believing and praying.

Compare that list with what Paul calls the fruit of the Spirit: "love, joy, peace, patience, kindness, goodness, faithfulness, gentleness, self-control." These are the qualities that God wants to produce in our lives, that He wants to see flowing out of our hearts. Fruit grows, and this particular fruit only grows through the work of the Holy Spirit within God's children.

Keep your new covenant heart pure before God, so that the flow of the rivers of living water remain unhindered. Then God will produce in you the fruit He desires to see, above all the love and faith that are outworking of His Spirit within you. Come back to the Cross again and again, tasting the love, mercy and forgiveness of your gracious Father. Know that it is He who will supply you with the grace to reach out to others in love, service, compassion, giving yourself willingly and joyfully for the delight of pleasing Him and furthering the work of His kingdom here on earth.

Your words of faith: "IF WE LOVE ONE ANOTHER, GOD ABIDES IN US AND HIS LOVE IS PERFECTED IN US."

30
Praise

TO BE FILLED with the Spirit is to be filled with praise for God. For praise is one of those "rivers of living water" that flows out of your heart.

David

Asking with faith will take place within the context of praise. David says:

> Bless the Lord, O my soul; and all that is within me, bless his holy name! Bless the Lord, O my soul, and forget not all his benefits, who forgives all your iniquity, who heals all your diseases, who redeems your life from the Pit, who crowns you with steadfast love and mercy, who satisfies you with good as long as you live (Ps. 103: 1–5).

David knew that the Lord whom he was blessing, or praising, was the God who was active in his life. He was not worshipping a remote being unidentified with his needs. Everything within him cried out in praise to the living God, because he knew the Lord's forgiveness and healing; His love, mercy and redemption; and His eternal goodness towards His children.

David knew, not only God's love for him, but for all His people. He tells *you* to praise God and be mindful of all His blessings, because:

He forgives all *your* iniquity;

He heals all *your* diseases;
He redeems *your* life from the Pit, from the deepest
darkness;
He crowns *you* with His perfect love and mercy;
He satisfies *you* with good as long as you live!

David didn't speak such words lightly. He knew what it
was to be afflicted, persecuted, oppressed, hemmed in on all
sides by his enemies; to feel separated from God, as if His
prayers were not being answered. And what is his response
in such circumstances? To PRAISE God.

I will bless the Lord at all times; his praise shall continually be in my mouth. My soul makes its boast in the
Lord; let the afflicted hear and be glad. O magnify
the Lord with me, and let us exalt his name together
(Ps. 34: 1–3).

Again, he does not speak only of his own practice. From
his experience of how God works he calls upon the
'afflicted', those in trouble, to join with him in praise: "O
magnify the Lord with me, and let us exalt his name
together." For he knows that God answers prayer; he sets
His people free from fear and saves them from all trouble.

I sought the Lord, and he answered me, and delivered
me from all my fears. Look to him, and be radiant; so
your faces shall never be ashamed The poor man
cried, and the Lord heard him, and saved him out of all
his troubles (Ps. 34: 4–6).

David knew what 'affliction' was all about; his life was
full of it. He also knew the faithfulness of his God: "Many
are the afflictions of the righteous; but the Lord delivers
him out of them all" (v. 19).

This is a statement of faith, based upon his own experience of clinging to the Word of his God, even when all the

circumstances around him seemed to point to disaster.
Psalm 71 will serve as a good example:

> In thee, O Lord, do I take refuge; let me never be put to
> shame!
> In thy righteousness deliver me and rescue me; incline
> thy ear to me, and save me!
> Be thou to me a rock of refuge, a strong fortress, to save
> me, for thou art my rock and my fortress.
> Rescue me, O my God, from the hand of the wicked,
> from the grasp of the unjust and cruel man.
> For thou, O Lord, art my hope, my trust, O Lord, from
> my youth.
> Upon thee I have leaned from birth; thou art he who
> took me from my mother's womb.
> My praise is continually of thee (Ps. 71: 1–6).

Asking and praising go together for David. He is not
afraid to lean on God, to come to Him and declare openly
and honestly his need. He does not look at the situation as
hopeless, because he knows the power and faithfulness of
God. He does not listen to the doubts that are fired at him,
but knows the Lord to be his trust.

> My enemies speak concerning me, those who watch for
> my life consult together and say, "God has forsaken
> him; pursue and seize him, for there is none to deliver
> him" (vv. 10–11).

David's answer is: "But I will hope continually, and will
praise thee yet more and more" (v. 14). God has not lost
control of his life. David belongs to Him. "Thou who hast
made me see many sore troubles wilt revive me again"
(v. 20). And the Psalm ends on a note of triumph:

> I will also praise thee with the harp for thy faith-
> fulness, O my God;

I will sing praises to thee with the lyre, O Holy One of
Israel.
My lips will shout for joy, when I sing praises to thee;
my soul also which thou hast rescued.
And my tongue will talk of thy righteous help all the
day long, for they have been put to shame and disgrace
who sought to do me hurt (vv. 22–24).

Those are words of faith, for they show that David believed the victory that had not yet happened! He was praying, believing that he had received it and knowing that it
would be his. So praise fills his heart, for he knows that God
will act to save him from his enemies.

The Psalms are rich in inspiration for faith. They do not
hide us from the deep yearnings of the heart, or the most
impossible of situations; and yet they are shot through with
praise for the faithful God of steadfast love.

David faithfully prays in the way that Jesus was to instruct his disciples centuries later. He addresses the 'mountains':

Depart from me, all you workers of evil; for the Lord
has heard the sound of my weeping. The Lord has
heard my supplication; the Lord accepts my prayer. All
my enemies shall be ashamed and sorely troubled; they
shall turn back, and be put to shame in a moment
(Ps. 6: 8–10).

Why could David be so certain, when circumstances
seemed to contradict such optimistic faith? Because GOD
HAD MADE A COVENANT with him.

The steadfast love of the Lord is from everlasting to
everlasting upon those who fear him, and his righteousness to children's children, to those who keep his covenant and remember to do his commandments (Ps.
103: 17–18).

He is mindful of his covenant for ever, of the word that he commanded, for a thousand generations (Ps. 105: 8).

And David remembered the covenant promises that he had been given by God. The Lord said:

I will not remove from him my steadfast love, or be false to my faithfulness. I will not violate my covenant or alter the word that went forth from my lips (Ps. 89: 33–34).

We are the new covenant children of God. He will be faithful to every promise that He has given us by Jesus. He will not violate the covenant that is in His blood. He will not alter one word spoken by His Son. So we can have boldness and confidence when we approach our Father, knowing that it is His purpose to answer us, to heal us and deliver us, to honour the word of Jesus: "If you ask anything in my name, I will do it."

We can come with praise for God, knowing that He will be faithful and true to His Word, that His love for us will never fail.

The Early Church

The church in Jerusalem, newly filled with the Holy Spirit, came together daily "praising God and having favour with all the people". It was at that time that "many wonders and signs were done through the apostles" (See Acts 2: 43–47). Faith led to the release of God's power among them.

And his name, by faith in his name, has made this man strong whom you see and know; and the faith which is through Jesus has given the man this perfect health in the presence of you all (Acts 3: 16).

Even in prison Paul and Silas "were praying and singing hymns to God". And what was the outcome of the combination of prayer and praise?

> And suddenly there was a great earthquake, so that the foundations of the prison were shaken; and immediately all the doors were open and everyone's fetters were unfastened (Acts 16: 26).

When you pray, ask with praise and thanksgiving because all your needs have already been met in Jesus. Paul begins his great passage in Ephesians, chapter 1, with the words:

> Blessed be the God and Father of our Lord Jesus Christ, who has blessed us in Christ with every spiritual blessing in the heavenly places (v. 3).

He *has* blessed us. As we come to our Father in faith, so we appropriate what He has already made available to us through His precious Son, who "by the power at work within us is able to do far more abundantly than all that we ask or think" (Eph. 3: 20).

Many Christians have discovered that praising God is not simply singing hymns or psalms with the mouth. That is an activity that goes on in many church buildings, without ever reaching the heights of real praise.

Praise starts deep within us. When filled with the Holy Spirit, people experience the praise that flows from the heart and lifts them into the company of the heavenly host that surrounds the throne of God with ceaseless praise.

> Through him (Jesus) then let us continually offer up a sacrifice of praise to God, that is, the fruit of those who acknowledge his name (Heb. 13: 15).

No matter what the situation, the flow of praise in our lives needs to be continuous, because God is always worthy of praise. When we come to Him to ask anything, we come to the one who deserves to be praised, worshipped and adored. And if we love Him that will be our joy.

Some people say that they feel hypocritical if they praise or worship God, without "feeling like it". This is to suggest that He should only be praised when we have the right feelings. That is obviously not right, for although feelings can easily change from one moment to the next, God does not change. Jesus is the same "yesterday, today and forever".

God the Father and God the Son are always worthy of praise in the power of God, the Holy Spirit.

The Value of Tongues

It is the Holy Spirit that comes to your aid when you feel unable to praise. You can use the prayer language, or tongue, that the Spirit gives you. As you allow the Spirit to pray in you and through you in this way, He will turn your attention to the Lord. When you begin to pray you may feel sorry for yourself, but in a few minutes you will be filled with the awe and wonder of knowing that you are before the throne of God in praise.

It is the language of praise because it is the language of the Spirit. Because you do understand the words you speak "in a tongue" it is easy to belittle this gift.

No gift of God should be under-rated. Paul valued it greatly. "I want you all to speak in tongues", he tells the Corinthians (I Cor. 14: 5); "I thank God that I speak in tongues more than you all" (v. 18). However, he was con-cerned to teach them the proper use of this gift, *in public*, "So, my brethren, earnestly desire to prophesy, and do not forbid speaking in tongues" (v. 39). During the course of public worship, prophesy is the better gift to use because that is God speaking to His people in their native language that can readily be understood by all.

However, Paul does not denigrate the gift of tongues. Far

from it; he values it highly and obviously used it extensively in his personal prayer and praise. "I will pray with the spirit and I will pray with the mind also; I will sing with the spirit and I will sing with the mind also" (vv. 13–15).

Give Yourself in Praise

We cannot talk of praying with faith without seeing all that God has made available to us for this purpose. We can praise Him with both mind and spirit. And praise builds faith because it directs our attention away from the 'mountains' and on to the One who has the power to move them. It releases His power into the situation, where before there may only have been fear or despair.

Many people who seek healing, go from one healing service to another hoping to receive their answer. Their need can easily claim their whole attention. Whenever they pray, much of the time is spent dwelling upon their own problem.

I have known many people to receive their healing, when they least expect it. While attending an act of worship where the people have been free to express their praise for God "in the Spirit", they have been caught up in the praise and have forgotten all about their needs. They have simply given themselves in worship to the Lord, whose Presence is so real. Then they discover that the healing has taken place, without anyone praying for them or ministering to them.

"It is more blessed to give than to receive," Jesus said. In giving you receive. Praise is giving to God the love and adoration of our hearts, no matter what our feelings or the circumstances in which we find ourselves. And He gives His Presence to us. "Pray at all times in the Spirit, with all prayer and supplication" (Eph. 6: 18).

Paul spoke of the importance of rejoicing, praising and thanking the Lord, no matter what the circumstances. "Rejoice always, pray constantly, give thanks in all circumstances; for this is the will of God in Christ Jesus for you"

(1 Thess. 5: 16–18). "Rejoice in the Lord always; again I will say, Rejoice" (Phil. 4: 4).

There will be many occasions when you won't feel like rejoicing. The last thing in the world you will want to do is praise the Lord. Those are occasions when you need to praise Him. That may require a big effort; you really have to make yourself sometimes. But it will never cease to amaze me how praise transforms a situation. The mountains look smaller! And God seems so much bigger!

Jude sums up much of what we have discovered about praying the prayer of faith:

> You beloved, build yourselves up on your most holy faith; pray in the Holy Spirit; keep yourselves in the love of God; wait for the mercy of our Lord Jesus Christ unto eternal life (Jude 20–21).

These verses bring together the words 'faith', 'pray', 'Holy Spirit', 'love', 'wait', and 'mercy'.

By His Holy Spirit, God wants to encourage faith within you. He wants to teach you to pray with faith, believing His promises. He wants that faith and prayer to come from a heart that is full of love and praise for Him. He wants you to learn to wait patiently until you see the fulfilment of the promise, that God has indeed had mercy upon you as the child He loves.

Your words of faith: "BLESS THE LORD, O MY SOUL AND ALL THAT IS WITHIN ME BLESS HIS HOLY NAME."

31

In Great Adversity

COUNT IT ALL joy, my brethren, when you meet various trials, for you know that the testing of your faith produces steadfastness. And let steadfastness have its full effect, that you may be perfect and complete, lacking in nothing (James 1: 2–4).

It is not easy to greet trials and difficulties with a sense of joy. You are more likely to feel angry, bitter and resentful, even towards God for allowing such trials in your life. Yet James knows that God lets these things happen so that our faith may be built up and made steadfast, dependable – like the love God has for us. Discovering that love in the midst of adversity is one of the greatest of human needs. The prophet, Habakkuk, demonstrates his faith in the face of great adversity:

Though the fig tree do not blossom, nor fruit be on the vines, the produce of the olive fail and the fields yield no food, the flock be cut off from the fold and there be no herd in the stalls, yet I will rejoice in the Lord, I will joy in the God of my salvation. God, the Lord, is my strength; he makes my feet like hinds' feet, he makes me tread upon my high places (Hab. 3: 17–19).

God is *your* Father, no matter how bad things are.

Jesus is *your* Saviour, no matter how desperate they appear.

The Holy Spirit fills *your* life and you can never be separated from the presence of God *within* you, even in the most dire situation.

As a new covenant child of God, He is your Father, your Saviour, your Counsellor and your Lord.

> The steadfast love of the Lord never ceases, his mercies never come to an end; they are new every morning; great is thy faithfulness. "The Lord is my portion," says my soul, "therefore I will hope in him." The Lord is good to those who wait for him, to the soul that seeks him (Lam. 3: 22–25).

Job

Satan was given leave by God to test the faith of Job, who is described as "a blameless and upright man, who fears God and turns away from evil" (1: 8). He lost his cattle, sheep, camels, servants and even his children. Yet "in all this Job did not sin or charge God with wrong" (1: 22).

Then Job was subjected to intense physical suffering, but still he "did not sin with his lips" (2: 10). Three friends came to "comfort" him. "They sat with him on the ground seven days and seven nights, and no one spoke a word to him, for they saw that his suffering was very great" (2: 13). They then proceeded to give him chapter after chapter of good advice.

This servant of God was on the receiving end of a three-fold battering.

1. He suffered because of what Satan did to him, his possessions and loved ones.

2. He suffered the criticism of his friends, who told him that he must be to blame for all that had befallen him.

3. He suffered as a result of his own fear: "For the thing that I fear comes upon me, and what I dread befalls me." He had been expecting trouble and he got it!

God does not promise us a life free from affliction and trial; but in Jesus, He has given us the victory over all the works of Satan. The Lord will never forsake the man whose trust is in Him.

Job was no longer able to trust in his wealth, the love of his children or the useless advice of his friends. His faith had to be in God alone. He said to the Lord: "I know that thou canst do all things, and that no purpose of thine can be thwarted" (44: 2).

And God proved faithful to His Servant. "And the Lord restored the fortunes of Job, when he had prayed for his friends; and the Lord gave Job twice as much as he had before,' (42: 10).

Even in his deprivation and loss, Job gave first by praying for his friends, useless though they had been with all their advice. And then God gave to him, "twice as much as he had before."

During a time of intense difficulty and stress it is not easy to hang on in faith. It seems that one's cries of desperation go unheard by God. There are friends with advice, but with no power to change the circumstances. And yet our covenant God is not deaf or blind to our needs.

Joseph

Joseph had two dreams, which clearly indicated that he would "have dominion over" his eleven brothers, all older than himself. Everything that happened to Joseph from that moment seemed to indicate the opposite. The older brothers decided first to kill him and then to sell him. Hardly a fulfilment of the promise given to Joseph in his dream!

He is taken to far away Egypt where he is sold as a servant, and thrown into prison on a false charge laid against him by his master's wife. Is that the fulfilment of the promise? It seems that the God of justice has deserted him, has forgotten him altogether. Is he to believe the circumstances, or the dream he has been given?

How do you hold on with faith, when you feel as if you

have been thrown into a deep pit, or treated unjustly by people, when you feel imprisoned by your situation? Joseph had to battle through all the adverse circumstances before he saw the promise fulfilled.

The Spirit's Prayer

When the going is tough and we find it really difficult to see how God is going to break through the problem, "the Spirit helps us in our weakness; for we do not know how to pray as we ought" (Rom. 8: 26).

The Spirit wants the Father's victory in every situation. There are times when we do not know what to pray with the mind. We will need to pray "with the Spirit", using the tongue, or language that God makes available to us. Through this gift the Spirit inspires the right words for the occasion, even though you cannot understand them. The answer to the need is beyond your understanding. No problem, however, is beyond the comprehension of the Holy Spirit, and He will pray the right words through you. Having prayed in tongues, you then pray again in your native language, asking God for the interpretation to the prayer that the Spirit has given you. In this way your mind is informed by the Spirit and becomes 'fruitful'. You know what to pray for more clearly; you understand the situation better.

If you have been filled with the Holy Spirit, the gift of 'tongues' is one of the resources that God has made available to you. Don't waste it, for every gift of the Holy Spirit is precious.

Even when you think your mind fully understands the situation, it is good to use the Spirit's language also. For God's wisdom is infinitely greater than yours; the Spirit always knows what to pray. Paul says:

I will pray with the spirit and I will pray with the mind

also; I will sing with the spirit and I will sing with the mind also (1 Cor. 14: 15).

Not the spirit *or* the mind; the spirit *and* the mind. "Pray at all times in the Spirit, with all prayer and supplication" (Eph. 6: 18).

Groans

There are occasions when "the Spirit himself intercedes for us with sighs too deep for words". In the depths of our despair He prays for us, not only from heaven, but in us. The Holy Spirit wants to direct us to the Father, to His love, to his promises and to inspire faith within us that, no matter how black the situation, God will honour His Word as we put our trust and confidence in Him.

> We know that in everything God works for good with those who love him, who are called according to his purpose (Rom. 8: 28).

There will be many situations in which you cannot understand the purpose of God; you cannot see why He should have allowed that particular problem to arise.

As you continue to look to Him, to set your mind on the things of the Spirit, to allow the Spirit to pray in you and through you and for you, to hold on to promises of your faithful Father, you will see His hand at work resolving the needs and giving understanding of His purpose.

> He who did not spare his own Son but gave him up for us all, will he not also give us all things with him? (Rom. 8: 32).

It does not matter what the situation.

In all these things we are more than conquerors

through him who loved us. For I am sure that neither death, nor life, nor angels, nor principalities, nor things present, nor things to come ... will be able to separate us from the love of God in Christ Jesus our Lord (Rom. 8: 37–39).

And that love is the Love that gives, the Love that cares, the Love that heals, the Love that will meet us where it hurts, where the need is.

Whenever the going is tough, it is hard to believe, to hold on to the promises. Remember, nothing can separate YOU from the love of God in Christ Jesus your Lord. NOTHING! "Nor things present, nor things to come." NOTHING!

When God speaks He does not fail to keep His Word. Joseph was vindicated, rose in the nation to be second only to the Pharaoh himself, and during the time of famine received his brothers, who bowed before him and begged to be allowed to buy food. As with Job, the Lord turned His adversity to great blessings and riches.

God is going to take you through your problem, to His rich purpose beyond.

Your words of faith: "THE STEADFAST LOVE OF THE LORD NEVER CEASES, HIS MERCIES NEVER COME TO AN END."

32

The Household of Faith

GOD INTENDS HIS children to be one. Loving one another.
Encouraging one another. Bearing one another's burdens.
Rejoicing together. Weeping together. Jesus prayed for all
those who would come to believe in Him, "that they may
become perfectly one, so that the world may know that thou
hast sent me and hast loved them, even as thou hast loved
me" (John 17: 23).

The very evidence of that love, will not be in our sermons
or doctrines, but in the quality of our life together that is
demonstrated to the world, in two ways in particular; the
way we love one another, and the way that we believe
together for God to answer our prayers.

The evidence of the Father's love for Jesus was seen in
their loving relationship and in the way that the Father
honoured the words and prayers of His Son, performing His
works through Him. No one man will reflect the perfect
love and power of Jesus. Those who believe in Him are
incorporated in the Body of Christ. It is through that Body
that the love, life and power of the Lord are to be ministered
to the world.

The unity of life among Christians is stressed time and
again in scripture. As members of the Body of Christ we are
"members one of another". We "belong to each other". We
are "one person in Christ Jesus". We are "branches" of the
Vine, so that the sap of God's Spirit can flow from branch to
branch and cause us to be fruitful.

Believing Together

It is not surprising, therefore that Jesus spoke about praying together in faith:

> Again I say to you, if two of you agree on earth about ANYTHING they ask, it WILL BE DONE FOR THEM by my Father in heaven (Matt. 18: 19).

There is that word again: 'ANYTHING'! Not 'some things' or a 'few things' or even 'many things', ANYTHING!

Jesus does not mean if any two of you agree the same verbal prayer, or form of words. It is not the words that matter, but the belief in the hearts of those who are praying.

He does not mean someone praying and everybody else saying 'Amen' at the end. There may be no 'agreeing' or unity of faith on occasions.

Jesus does mean that if any two of you agree to pray "in my name"; that you agree to pray as if Jesus Himself is asking, with His faith and His expectancy, believing that you have received it. Then "it will be done for them by my Father in heaven".

There can be great value in praying the prayer of faith with others who will believe with you until you see the promise fulfilled. Together you can reject the doubts when they assail you, and refuse to believe the circumstances against the promises of your loving and faithful Father. Believing together.

"For where two or three gathered in my name, there am I in the midst of them" (Matt 18: 20). If you are gathered "in my name", Jesus is present to pray along with you, and you with Him. His Presence can inspire faith and expectancy in your hearts, as you look together with Him to your Father. You are agreeing with Jesus in this prayer. AND HE IS AGREEING WITH YOU.

Talk Together

Again it needs to be emphasised how important it can be for Christians, whether praying in two's and three's or in larger groups, to talk together first before they pray; talk about what they believe God will do in answer to their prayer. Discover what their faith and expectancy is, or needs to be.

Perhaps this will mean that the members of the group will need to minister to one another. Perhaps some will have to confess doubt and bring that to the Lord. He does not condemn us for our doubts. What matters to Him above all else, is that we are prepared to be open and honest with Him.

Obviously within the context of a large number of people praying (a whole congregation, for example) it is not always possible to do this before praying. But faith of the kind that Jesus talks about, should never be assumed by those who are responsible for the leading of worship or the conducting of large prayer meetings. A very short time of teaching should be possible on some occasions, reminding people that they are children of the new covenant, looking to their Father to honour His promises. And a short time can be spent in which those present can silently bring their fears, anxieties and doubts to the Lord before the prayer of faith is prayed together.

Some will need to be assured that any doubts that may be afflicting them will not 'spoil' the prayer. Jesus says: 'if TWO of you agree . . .", not a whole congregation! The more positive the faith, the greater the power there will be in the praying capacity of that body of people.

Learning to pray with faith can best be done in small groups, meeting in the informality of a home. It is there that you will feel more relaxed and able to share your fears and doubts, your problems and needs. It is within such groups that you can best learn to 'receive' the promises (see chapter 10). It is there that you can best learn to pray the prayer of faith with one another and for one another, as well as for others outside the group. Instead of praying and "hoping for the best", you can begin to believe together and be an encouragement to one answer during the time of 'waiting' for the 'tortoise' answers.

Answers

Whether in the congregation or prayer group, large or small, formal or informal, encourage one another by sharing week by week the answers received through prayer. As the faith of the congregation or group grows, so there will be more and greater answers to give thanks for. That faith will depend upon the openness of the congregation or group to the faith-inspiring work of the Holy Spirit, for it is His ministry to witness the words and promises of Jesus to our hearts.

But answered prayer also encourages faith. As we see God is faithful in honouring even our 'little faith', we learn to trust Him for bigger and greater things. You even learn to trust Him for your own needs. These answers to prayer are also a witness to others. They testify to the fact that God really does love His people and care about them by meeting their needs.

When there is 'Jesus faith' in a congregation, it will not be possible to announce the answer to every prayer. A selection will need to be made, not only of great miracles, but also of the answers to everyday needs. These will be an encouragement to those starting out on the way of faith. They will understand that God is concerned about everyday problems and situations; He does not only deal in mighty miracles! Extravagant claims on the one hand, and pettiness on the other should be avoided.

There does not need to be a prolonged time of personal testimony. The leader can simply give thanks to God for the answers received, giving only brief details, when that is more appropriate. And remember 'tortoise' answers are just as important as 'rockets' and will be an encouragement to others who are waiting.

The Ministering Body

Is any one among you suffering? Let him pray.
Is any cheerful? Let him sing praises.
Is any among you sick? Let him call for the elders of the church, and let them pray over him anointing him with oil in the name of the Lord; and the PRAYER OF FAITH WILL SAVE THE SICK MAN, and the Lord will raise him up; and if he has committed sins, he will be forgiven.
Therefore confess your sins to one another, and pray for one another, that you may be healed.
The prayer of a righteous man has great power in its effects (James 5: 13–16).

Those who suffer are to pray – with faith, of course, as Jesus teaches. Those who are cheerful are to sing praises.

The sick are to ask for ministry that they may be healed – not given piles of good advice and loads of sympathy. The prayer of faith will save the sick man from the disease that afflicts him. The Lord will raise him from his bed of sickness.

James gives us a good picture of the "household of faith" in action, praying with one another, ministering in faith to each other. A praising people. Openly and honestly confessing their faults to one another, and knowing the forgiveness of God.

No wonder we find the going tough if we try to "go it alone". God has provided for us a fellowship of believers, that together we may come to the Lord and see the fulfilment of His Promises. The sad thing is that this picture of the praying, believing, ministering church is so different from what is often found today.

Congregations often pray for the sick, but do not necessarily understand what it is to pray the prayer of faith that will heal the sick man. Some are not aware of the resources of the Holy Spirit that are available to them, to enable them to pray effectively.

Sick people often battle alone and do not call for the elders. Perhaps they do not believe anything would happen if they did. Perhaps the elders would not know what to do if they were called.

We need not despair! God has not given up on His Church, and He never will. If there is not 'faith-full' fellowship to support you in your local congregation, hold on to the last part of this passage: "The prayer of a righteous man has great power in its effects."

The Healing Sacrament

Why should there be so much sickness among Christian people? Paul gives the Corinthians an answer: because they do not believe the power of Jesus in the healing sacrament of His Body and Blood, the 'Holy Communion' or 'Eucharist' (the 'Thanksgiving').

> For anyone who eats and drinks without discerning the body eats and drinks judgment upon himself. That is why many of you are weak and ill, and some have died (1 Cor. 11: 29–30).

They were not believing the words: "This is my body which is given for you." "This cup is the new covenant in my blood."

If they had believed them, they would have come properly prepared and not with the casual approach they obviously had. So Paul warns them:

Whoever therefore, eats the bread or drinks the cup of the Lord in an unworthy manner will be guilty of profaning the body of the Lord. Let a man examine himself, and so eat of the bread and drink of the cup (1 Cor. 11: 27-28).

The sacrament was not a piece of magic that would automatically solve their problems and meet their needs. It was to be approached with faith.

In the sacrament of Holy Communion we have the opportunity of 'discern' the body and blood of the Lord. If it is regarded simply as a memorial of a past event, it will seem lifeless and powerless. If people believe that in some mystical way Jesus is conveying His Presence to His children, then it is the opportunity for them to believe that they will receive the healing and life that they need in response to their prayers of faith.

The Eucharist can be for you a meeting with the Lord. It is the opportunity for you to offer yourself to Him afresh. (The Offertory always precedes the sharing of the bread and wine; the giving before the receiving!) It is the ideal time to pray your prayer of faith, and let it be sealed with the "new covenant in my blood."

It is the occasion when you not only come to Jesus, but He comes and gives Himself afresh to you, in the way you need to receive Him, to bring His life into your need.

In times of sickness, when it is extremely difficult to pray, the sacramental acts of the laying on of hands, of anointing, and of the Holy Communion are God's provision, through the ministry of His Body, for your needs. Make full use of them, for God has much to give you through them.

Your words of faith: "IF TWO OF YOU AGREE ON EARTH ABOUT ANYTHING THEY ASK, IT WILL BE DONE FOR THEM BY MY FATHER IN HEAVEN."

33

Exciting Future

ALL OF US have to face the future; it is better to do so with trust in Jesus' words, than be the victim of your own fears and doubts. Faith is believing a Lord that you do not see, trusting Him to accomplish things that are as yet unseen.

> Now faith is the assurance of things hoped for, the conviction of things not seen (Heb. 11: 1).

The 'assurance' of things hoped for. When you pray, you want God to do what you ask. That is your hope. Hope becomes faith when you have that assurance in your heart that God will do it. Because:

You are His new covenant child;

He loves you and wants to give to you;

He will keep His promises;

He will be glorified in answering your prayers;

He wants your "joy to be full".

Faith is "the conviction of things not seen", the certainty in your heart that, although at the time of praying you cannot see the answer, yet with the eyes of faith you do see it. It will happen. God will do it.

Jesus said to Thomas:

> Have you believed because you have seen me? Blessed are those who have not seen and yet believe (John 20: 29).

I have not pretended that it is always easy to walk by faith; but it is exciting.

Often you will feel that God is asking you to step out of the boat on to the water. As you keep your trust in Him, it will be as rock beneath your feet. James says: "Faith by itself, if it has no works, is dead." Those are the works of faith that he is speaking of.

Like Noah, Abraham, Moses and all the men of faith in the Bible, the Lord will ask you to do things that will test, stretch and strengthen your faith. As a new covenant child, you are pledged to obedience to the Lord. It will not only be your faith that is tested, but your obedience too. And that means God is seeing whether you really love him.

The flood only came after Noah had built the ark in faith.

Abraham did not receive his inheritance until he had obeyed God and left his homeland.

Naaman, the commander of the Syrian army, was not healed of his leprosy until he had obediently washed seven times in the river Jordan.

Elijah challenged the prophets of Baal to the contest on Mount Carmel because he trusted the Lord's word to him that He would send rain.

Shadrach, Meshach and Abednego asserted positively, "our God is able to deliver us from the burning fiery furnace" before Nebuchadnezzar had them thrown into the flames.

Jesus told the ten lepers to go and show themselves to the priests; and they were healed as they obeyed His instruction.

The blind man in John, Chapter 9, did not receive his sight until he had gone and washed in the pool of Siloam, in obedience to Jesus.

And so on. The examples of faith are innumerable in the Bible. But there are these common features; the men of faith listened to the words of God and of His Son and obeyed them. They put their trust and confidence in Him rather than believe the circumstances, which were often desperate.

It is that walk of faith to which Jesus calls you. He will not test you beyond your capacity to believe. Yet He wants to show you how much more you can see of Him at work in your life when you exercise fully that faith He has already given you.

Often you will want to sit back and suggest to the Lord that He works the whole situation out for you. And just as often He will show you that the problems will only be resolved when you step out in faith first, obeying what He says and proving what you are truly believing Him to do.

Ahead of You

Yes, many exciting times lay ahead of you as you pray the prayer of faith. Many testing times. Many wonderful times, as you see the faithfulness of your Father.

There will be some failures – whenever you fail to trust and believe; whenever you stop giving and lapse back into only wanting to receive; whenever you allow sin and disobedience to spoil your relationship with God; whenever you fail to forgive others.

God will even use those failures. I thank Him that He allows me to fail whenever I put my trust in myself, rather than in Him. My failures indicate my need to be more generous and full of faith in my giving. I thank Him because he can use the opportunity to point out some area of disobedience in my life, or something that is not completely yielded to Him; or that there is something that needs to be put right with someone.

God does not answer the prayers only of the spiritual giants, but of ordinary folk like us. Those who are prepared to give themselves to Him and live for Him.

If you have not yet done the exercise outlined in Chapter 8, turn back and read it again. Give everything to God and you can then be confident and expectant that He will give everything to you.

Faith in the person of Jesus to heal and meet needs was high during His lifetime. It would be easy for us to say that the level of faith is not so high today, and that is why we do not see so many instantaneous miracles. There is truth in this, borne out by the number of people that are instantly healed at services where their faith in Jesus to act immediately, has been quickened.

I could have included many accounts of actual healings and answers to prayer, many of them instantaneous. I have not done so for two reasons. First, not everybody receives instant answers and the 'tortoises' are as important as the 'rockets'. Secondly, the illustrations of the teaching in this book need to come from your own life. They need to be the answers God gives *you* to *your* prayers.

Write and tell me about them; they will encourage me. Answers always do.

What I have written here I try to live out myself, and could tell you of many wonderful gifts received from my Father, some big things, many smaller ones. But I won't.

What I will share with you is the agony that I sometimes experience, holding on to the promises when nothing appears to be happening, when everything appears to be going wrong. Its an agony you often can't share with others; but it goes on deep inside you.

Yet there is always the thrill of the Spirit of God declaring those words of Jesus to my heart, in the face of all the difficulties. We'll share them together once more:

> Whatever you ask in my name, I WILL DO IT, that the Father may be glorified in the Son (John 14: 13).
> If you ask anything in my name, I WILL DO IT (John 14: 14).
> If you abide in me, and my words abide in you, ask whatever you will, and IT SHALL BE DONE FOR YOU (John 15: 7).
> Truly, truly, I say to you, if you ask anything of the Father, HE WILL GIVE IT TO YOU in my name (John 16: 23).
> Ask, and YOU WILL RECEIVE, that your joy may be full (John 16: 24).

Whatever you ask in prayer, believe that you have received it, and IT WILL BE YOURS (Mark 11: 24).
Ask, and IT WILL BE GIVEN YOU (Matt. 7: 7).
Again I say to you, if two of you agree on earth about anything they ask, IT WILL BE DONE for them by my Father in heaven (Matt. 18: 19).
Whatever you ask in prayer, YOU WILL RECEIVE, if you have faith (Matt. 21: 22).

There can be no doubt that it is God's purpose to give you whatever you ask in faith. IT WILL BE DONE. IT WILL BE GIVEN. Over and over again Jesus repeats the same promise.

Praise God for all the instantaneous answers to prayer. Praise Him for all those that involve faithful, patient enduring until the promise is received.

And once again we need to affirm positively that Jesus is talking about 'anything' or 'whatever' we ask:

> WHATEVER you ask in my name . . . (John 14: 13).
> If you ask ANYTHING . . . (John 14: 14).
> . . . ask WHATEVER YOU WILL . . . (John 15: 7).
> . . . if you ask anything of the Father . . . (John 16: 23).
> WHATEVER you ask in prayer . . . (Mark 11: 24).
> . . . if two of you agree on earth about ANYTHING they ask . . . (Matt. 18: 19).
> WHATEVER you ask in prayer . . . (Matt. 21: 22).

Jesus promises the answer to ALL your prayers of faith. Every one!

I said just now that the answers to prayer encourage me, and so they do. But I have to honestly say that the promises of Jesus encourage me more. For there is always more to receive from our Father. And that means more opportunities to give first and have my faith deepened, stretched, extended. To see those promises more completely fulfilled in my life.

Use This Book

Now that you have read this book, go back over it again and again. Spend time on each chapter absorbing the teaching and receiving the words of faith so that they become part of you. And put those words to work in your asking prayer.

If you have found it helpful, give this book to others. There are many people around you who need God to answer them; other Christian friends, those you meet at church, your neighbours, at work and at home.

That word 'give' will be very important to you as you learn to pray with faith. Use every opportunity to give and expect God to give back to you "good measure, pressed down, shaken together, running over".

> Seek first his kingdom and his righteousness, and all these things will be yours as well (Matt. 6: 33).

It's staggering, but its true. God loves you and wants to give you His best. "If YOU ask anything in my name, I will do it" (John 14: 14).

Yes, YOU!

Your words of faith: "SEEK FIRST HIS KINGDOM AND HIS RIGHTEOUSNESS. AND ALL THESE THINGS SHALL BE YOURS AS WELL."

Appendix: Your Words of Faith

1. "If you ask anything in my name, I will do it."
2. "He did all that the Lord commanded him."
3. "Is anything too hard for the Lord?"
4. "I will be your God and you shall be my people."
5. "You are a God ready to forgive, gracious and merciful, slow to anger and abounding in steadfast love."
6. "A new heart I will give you and a new Spirit I will put within you."
7. "I have been crucified with Christ."
8. "It is no longer I who live, but Christ who lives in me."
9. "I will put my Spirit within you, and you shall live."
10. "Heaven and earth will pass away, but my words will not pass away."
11. "My words . . . are life to he who finds them and healing to all his flesh."
12. "You are precious in my eyes, and honoured, and I love you."
13. "If you abide in me, and my words abide in you, ask whatever you will and it shall be done for you."
14. "You did not choose me, but I chose you and appointed you that you should go and bear fruit and that your fruit should abide; so that whatever you ask the Father in my name he may give it to you."
15. "Have faith in God."
16. "Nothing will be impossible for you."
17. "Whatever you ask in prayer, believe that you have received it, and it will be yours."
18. "It will be yours." "It will be given you." "It will be done for you."
19. "Whatever you ask in my name, I will do it."
20. "Ask, and you will receive, that your joy may be full."
21. "Your Father knows what you need before you ask him."
22. "Go; be it done for you as you have believed."
23. "He took our infirmities and bore our diseases."

24. "Take heart, my son; your sins are forgiven you." "Take heart, daughter; your faith has made you well."
25. "Do you believe I am able to do this?"
26. "Through God you are no longer a slave but a son, and if a son then an heir."
27. "Give and it shall be given to you; good measure, pressed down, shaken together, running over, will be put into your lap. For the measure you give will be the measure you get back."
28. "Hearing the word, hold it fast in an honest and good heart, and bring forth fruit with patience."
29. "If we love one another, God abides in us and his love is perfected in us."
30. "Bless the Lord, O my soul, and all that is within me bless his holy name."
31. "The steadfast love of the Lord never ceases, his mercies never come to an end."
32. "If two of you agree on earth about anything they ask, it will be done for them by my Father in heaven."
33. "Seek first his kingdom and his righteousness, and all these things shall be yours as well."

HODDER CHRISTIAN ESSENTIALS

- **Esteemed Authors**
- **Essential Subjects**
- **Excellent Value**

***Anything You Ask* by Colin Urquhart**
How to pray in faith

***Baptism* by Michael Green**
Its purpose, practice and power

***Beyond Ourselves* by Catherine Marshall**
Our relationship with God

***The Empty Cross of Jesus* by Michael Green**
The crucifixion and resurrection

***Fear No Evil* by David Watson**
Faith in the face of death

***The Gift of Giving* by R T Kendall**
What it means to tithe

***God has Spoken* by J I Packer**
Reading God's word

***The Gravedigger Files* by Os Guinness**
The threats facing the Church

***The Hard Sayings of Jesus* by F F Bruce**
Explaining the most difficult gospel sayings

***The Helper* by Catherine Marshall**
The work of the Holy Spirit

***I Am Not Ashamed* by Martin Lloyd-Jones**
Rejoicing in the good news of the gospel

***Loving God* by Charles Colson**
Obeying the first commandment

***One in the Spirit* by David Watson**
The work of the Holy Spirit

***Out of the Rut, Into Revival* by A W Tozer**
The need for renewal, and how to find it

***Prayers and Promises for Every Day* by Corrie ten Boom**
The fulfilment of God's promises in our lives

***This Day is the Lord's* by Corrie ten Boom**
Daily meditations to renew our faith